Consciousness and Perception

Teddy Black

Published by Teddy Black, 2024.

While every precaution has been taken in the preparation of this book, the publisher assumes no responsibility for errors or omissions, or for damages resulting from the use of the information contained herein.

CONSCIOUSNESS AND PERCEPTION

First edition. November 6, 2024.

Copyright © 2024 Teddy Black.

ISBN: 979-8227996909

Written by Teddy Black.

Introduction: The Enigma of Consciousness

Consciousness is at the heart of human experience—a fundamental yet elusive force that defines what it means to be aware. It shapes my thoughts, emotions, and sensations, creating a tapestry of perceptions that bring color and meaning to life. Despite its centrality, consciousness remains one of psychology's greatest mysteries, defying simple explanations and inviting questions that probe the boundaries of human understanding. What is consciousness, and why does it exist? How does it transform raw sensory input into meaningful experiences? This book explores these questions, examining consciousness as both a scientific phenomenon and a deeply personal experience that bridges the gap between mind and world.

From ancient philosophy to modern neuroscience, the study of consciousness has fascinated thinkers across time. While science has illuminated aspects of the brain and perception, it has yet to uncover the full nature of subjective awareness. This enigma, often referred to as the "hard problem" of consciousness, points to a gap in understanding that leaves room for wonder and speculation. For me, this mystery is not just an academic puzzle; it is an invitation to explore the depths of my own mind, understanding consciousness as a dynamic experience that shapes how I interact with the world and myself. Through this exploration, I hope to gain insight into the nature of reality, the potential of perception, and the intricate dance between mind and body.

Consciousness: A Spectrum of Awareness

Consciousness is not a single, fixed state; it exists on a spectrum that ranges from simple awareness to complex introspective thought. At the most basic level, consciousness allows me to recognize my surroundings and respond to them—a level of awareness shared by many animals and even certain artificial systems. Moving up this spectrum, consciousness includes self-awareness, the ability to reflect on my own existence and ponder my thoughts and emotions. This self-reflective capacity allows me to not only perceive but also interpret and analyze my experiences, creating a sense of identity that is both stable and evolving.

By viewing consciousness as a spectrum, I gain a fuller understanding of its versatility and depth. This perspective suggests that consciousness is not limited to humans but is instead a continuum of experiences that can be found across species and even within artificial systems that mimic certain aspects of awareness. This spectrum of consciousness, from basic sensory awareness to higher-order introspection, reveals that consciousness is a fluid phenomenon, capable of adapting and evolving in response to different contexts and levels of complexity. For me, this understanding enriches my view of consciousness, showing it to be a dynamic force that permeates life in ways that are both familiar and profound.

The Constructed Nature of Perception

One of the most fascinating aspects of consciousness is its role in constructing reality through perception. My senses collect data from the environment, but it is my mind that interprets and organizes this data into a cohesive experience. This process of interpretation means that perception is not a straightforward reflection of reality; it is a subjective construct shaped by past experiences, emotions, and expectations. When I see a familiar face or place, my perception is colored by memories and associations that go beyond mere sensory input, creating a reality that is uniquely my own.

The constructive nature of perception highlights the flexibility of consciousness. While my senses provide the raw material for experience, my mind actively shapes how I interpret and understand the world. This process shows that consciousness is not a passive observer; it is an active participant in creating reality, filtering and framing each experience according to personal and contextual factors. For me, this insight into perception reveals that reality is a blend of objective data and subjective interpretation, inviting me to question my assumptions and remain open to alternative perspectives.

The Intersection of Science and Philosophy

The study of consciousness lies at the intersection of science and philosophy, where empirical research meets existential inquiry. Neuroscientists approach consciousness by studying the brain, mapping neural networks, and examining the processes that produce awareness. Through techniques such as brain imaging, scientists have gained insights into the biological underpinnings of consciousness, identifying regions and pathways that are crucial for perception, memory, and emotion. This scientific approach provides a framework for understanding how consciousness operates on a physical level, grounding awareness in the brain's complex architecture.

Philosophers, however, ask questions that go beyond biology, probing the nature of consciousness itself. Is consciousness a purely material phenomenon, or does it contain elements that transcend the physical? Some philosophers argue for dualism, suggesting that consciousness exists independently of the body, while others propose a monistic view, where consciousness is fully rooted in physical processes. This philosophical debate raises questions about free will, personal identity, and the potential for consciousness beyond the confines of the brain. For me, this intersection between science and philosophy enriches the study of consciousness, revealing it as a phenomenon that is as much about meaning and self-understanding as it is about biology.

Why Consciousness Matters

Consciousness is more than an abstract concept; it is the essence of personal experience, defining how I interact with the world, form relationships, and pursue meaning. Every thought, emotion, and sensation is filtered through consciousness, creating a narrative that connects each moment into a coherent whole. Consciousness shapes my values, guides my decisions, and provides a sense of continuity that ties my past to my present and future. Without consciousness, life would be a series of disconnected events, devoid of the depth and richness that make existence meaningful.

For me, consciousness matters because it is the foundation of self-awareness and personal growth. It allows me to reflect on my experiences, learn from my mistakes, and strive for a better understanding of myself and the world. This capacity for reflection is what makes consciousness transformative, giving me the tools to approach life with intention, curiosity, and empathy. By exploring consciousness, I hope to deepen my connection to myself and others, gaining insight into the nature of human experience and the potential for growth and understanding.

The Journey into Consciousness

This book is an invitation to journey into the depths of consciousness, exploring its foundations, limitations, and possibilities. Each chapter examines a different aspect of awareness, from the mind-body connection to altered states of consciousness, revealing the complexity and richness of the mind. Through this exploration, I seek to understand not only the mechanisms of consciousness but also its potential to expand and evolve. Consciousness, I believe, is not a static state; it is an ever-changing experience that reflects my engagement with life and my pursuit of meaning.

As I delve into the mysteries of consciousness, I approach it as both a scientific inquiry and a personal exploration. Consciousness is, after all, the essence of who I am, shaping every aspect of my existence. By studying its nature and dynamics, I hope to gain a deeper understanding of myself, finding ways to enhance my perception, cultivate awareness, and embrace the unknown. This journey is a celebration of consciousness, an exploration of the mind's potential, and an invitation to see life through the lens of awareness.

Reflections on the Enigma of Consciousness

Consciousness remains one of the greatest mysteries of human existence, a phenomenon that defies easy explanation yet is central to every aspect of life. By exploring consciousness, I embark on a journey that bridges science, philosophy, and personal experience, seeking to understand the nature of awareness and its role in shaping reality. This journey is an invitation to question, reflect, and grow, recognizing that consciousness is not just a state of awareness but a dynamic process that evolves with each new experience.

For me, the enigma of consciousness is a reminder that life is a journey of discovery, one that invites me to look beyond the surface and explore the depths of the mind. By embracing the mystery, I open myself to the unknown, finding meaning in the questions that remain unanswered. This book is a celebration of consciousness, an exploration of its many facets, and a testament to the wonder of existence. As I move forward, I carry with me a sense of curiosity, knowing that consciousness will always hold new layers to uncover and new insights to explore.

Chapter 1: The Enigma of Consciousness

Consciousness is a profound mystery, one that has puzzled thinkers for centuries. It is the essence of what it means to be aware, shaping every moment of my experience and giving depth to my understanding of reality. Consciousness encompasses everything from my thoughts and emotions to my sensations and memories, creating a continuous stream of awareness that connects me to the world. Despite its central role in human experience, consciousness remains elusive, defying full scientific explanation. In this chapter, I begin to explore the questions that define consciousness: What is it? How does it arise? And why does it shape my experience so profoundly?

The Basic Mystery of Consciousness

At its core, consciousness is the state of being aware. It is the ability to perceive, think, and feel, allowing me to engage with the world in a deeply personal way. However, while the effects of consciousness are evident in my daily life, its nature is harder to define. Unlike physical phenomena, consciousness cannot be directly measured or observed; it is an internal experience, unique to each individual. This makes consciousness one of psychology's greatest mysteries, raising questions about how subjective awareness arises from biological processes. For me, this mystery adds a sense of wonder to my understanding of the mind, suggesting that there may be aspects of existence that lie beyond what science can fully explain.

The basic mystery of consciousness is often referred to as the "hard problem"—a term coined by philosopher David Chalmers to describe the challenge of explaining how physical processes in the brain produce subjective experience. While scientists can study brain activity and map neural pathways, they cannot directly observe consciousness itself. This gap between physical processes and subjective awareness is at the heart of the enigma, suggesting that consciousness may have properties that are not easily reduced to material explanations. For me, this mystery invites curiosity and exploration, opening up questions about the nature of reality and the role of consciousness within it.

Consciousness as a Bridge Between Mind and World

One of the most remarkable aspects of consciousness is its role as a bridge between my inner thoughts and the external world. Through perception, I am able to interpret sensory information, turning raw data into meaningful experiences. Each sight, sound, taste, and touch is processed by my mind, creating a cohesive picture of reality that allows me to navigate life. This bridge between mind and world is not just a passive process; it actively shapes my understanding of existence, connecting my inner awareness with the environment in a way that is both dynamic and interactive.

Consciousness allows me to engage with the world on multiple levels, from the sensory details of my surroundings to the abstract concepts that give life meaning. For example, when I see a familiar place, my consciousness integrates the visual input with my memories, emotions, and personal associations, creating an experience that is uniquely mine. This ability to bridge the gap between mind and world is central to the richness of human experience, allowing me to interpret reality in ways that are personal and deeply resonant. For me, consciousness is not just a state of awareness—it is a living process that connects my inner self with the vastness of the external world.

Exploring the Scope of Consciousness

Consciousness exists on a spectrum, ranging from basic sensory awareness to complex introspective thought. At its simplest, consciousness allows me to be aware of my surroundings, responding to stimuli in ways that support survival. This basic level of consciousness is shared by many living organisms, each with its own way of interacting with the environment. As consciousness becomes more complex, it encompasses higher-order abilities such as self-reflection, imagination, and empathy. These abilities allow me to think beyond immediate needs, exploring abstract ideas and considering perspectives beyond my own.

At the highest levels, consciousness involves the ability to question existence itself, pondering concepts such as purpose, meaning, and morality. This reflective capacity is unique to humans, enabling personal growth, creativity, and the pursuit of knowledge. For me, this scope of consciousness reveals its versatility, showing that it is not a single, static state but a continuum of experiences that can expand or contract depending on awareness and focus. By exploring the scope of consciousness, I gain a fuller understanding of my own mind, recognizing that awareness is a journey of discovery that invites me to explore both the known and the unknown aspects of existence.

Theories on the Origins of Consciousness

CONSCIOUSNESS AND PERCEPTION

The origins of consciousness are a subject of ongoing debate, with theories from biology, philosophy, and psychology offering different perspectives. Biologically, consciousness is thought to arise from complex neural networks in the brain, with millions of neurons working together to produce awareness. This view suggests that consciousness is an emergent property, arising from the interactions of simpler processes to create a unified experience. According to this theory, consciousness is rooted in the brain's physical structure, with each sensory experience contributing to the construction of a coherent self.

Philosophers, however, offer alternative theories, questioning whether consciousness can be fully explained by physical processes alone. Some suggest that consciousness may be a fundamental property of the universe, similar to space and time. This view, known as panpsychism, proposes that all matter has some degree of consciousness, with human awareness representing a higher level of complexity. For me, the range of theories on consciousness reveals the depth of the mystery, showing that awareness may be a complex phenomenon that cannot be reduced to a single explanation. This exploration of origins opens up questions about the nature of existence, suggesting that consciousness may be both deeply rooted in the brain and intricately connected to the universe.

The Role of Consciousness in Shaping Reality

Consciousness does more than interpret reality—it actively shapes it. My perception, beliefs, and emotions influence how I see the world, creating a reality that is both personal and dynamic. When I am happy, the world seems brighter; when I am anxious, it feels more threatening. These shifts in perception reveal the extent to which consciousness is an active participant in creating reality, shaping each moment based on my internal state. This ability to shape reality through perception highlights the subjective nature of consciousness, showing that my experience of the world is a reflection of my inner thoughts and feelings.

This active role of consciousness suggests that reality is not purely objective; it is a co-creation between my mind and the external environment. For me, this realization is both empowering and humbling, as it reveals the influence I have over my own experience while also acknowledging the limitations of perception. Consciousness, therefore, is not a passive observer; it is a force that shapes how I engage with life, offering me the opportunity to approach each experience with intention and awareness. By understanding the role of consciousness in shaping reality, I learn to view life as a creative process, one that invites me to explore my potential and expand my understanding of existence.

The Paradox of Self-Awareness

One of the most intriguing aspects of consciousness is self-awareness—the ability to reflect on one's own thoughts and experiences. Self-awareness allows me to think about who I am, what I value, and where I am going, creating a sense of identity that is both stable and evolving. This reflective capacity is a defining feature of human consciousness, setting it apart from other forms of awareness. However, self-awareness also introduces a paradox: the more I understand myself, the more I realize there is to learn. This endless journey of self-discovery is both liberating and challenging, as it reveals the depth and complexity of consciousness.

Self-awareness invites me to question my beliefs, re-evaluate my assumptions, and explore new perspectives, creating a continuous process of growth. Yet, this process also reveals the limitations of self-knowledge, as there are always aspects of myself that remain hidden or unexplored. For me, this paradox of self-awareness is a reminder that consciousness is both a gift and a challenge, offering me the opportunity to understand myself while also revealing the vastness of the mind. This dual nature of self-awareness encourages me to approach consciousness with humility, recognizing that true understanding is a lifelong journey.

Reflections on the Enigma of Consciousness

The enigma of consciousness is one of life's greatest mysteries, touching every aspect of human experience. From the basic awareness of the environment to the depths of self-reflection, consciousness shapes how I see the world and my place within it. Each perspective—from biology and philosophy to the study of self-awareness—adds a layer of complexity to my understanding, showing that consciousness is a phenomenon that defies simple explanation. For me, exploring the enigma of consciousness is not just an intellectual pursuit; it is a journey into the heart of existence, one that invites me to question, reflect, and grow.

This chapter is a reminder that consciousness is more than a state of awareness; it is an evolving experience that connects me to both the internal

CONSCIOUSNESS AND PERCEPTION

and external world. By embracing the mystery of consciousness, I open myself to the unknown, recognizing that there are always new depths to explore and new insights to uncover. In the journey to understand consciousness, I find a sense of wonder that enriches my life, revealing that the mind is not only a tool for navigating reality but also a gateway to the mysteries of existence.

Chapter 2: The Foundations of Consciousness

Consciousness is one of the most profound and mysterious aspects of human existence. It encompasses everything from basic sensory awareness to complex introspective thought, creating a spectrum of experiences that define how I perceive and interact with the world. While the origins and mechanisms of consciousness are still debated, various theories from biology, philosophy, and psychology offer insights into its foundations. These perspectives explore how consciousness emerges, what it encompasses, and why understanding its range is essential to grasping the nature of perception. In reflecting on the foundations of consciousness, I begin to see it as both a fundamental aspect of life and an evolving experience shaped by awareness, sensation, and thought.

Biological Perspectives on Consciousness

Biologists often approach consciousness as a product of neural processes within the brain. According to this perspective, consciousness arises from the interactions of neurons and the complex networks they form, creating a cohesive experience from various sensory inputs. The brain integrates information from the senses, processes it, and produces a unified perception of reality. This neural foundation suggests that consciousness is not a single entity but rather an emergent property—a result of countless smaller processes working together to create a continuous, self-aware experience.

The biological perspective on consciousness highlights the role of brain regions, such as the cerebral cortex and the thalamus, in maintaining awareness. These areas are believed to act as hubs for integrating sensory data, filtering it to create a coherent view of the world. For me, this view of consciousness as a biological phenomenon underscores the connection between mind and body, showing that awareness is deeply rooted in physical processes. By understanding the brain's role in creating consciousness, I gain insight into how mental states are linked to neural activity, revealing a layer of consciousness that is both structured and fluid, shaped by the brain's intricate design.

Philosophical Views on the Nature of Consciousness

Philosophers have long explored the nature of consciousness, questioning whether it is purely material or if it contains elements beyond physical processes. Some, like René Descartes, argue for a dualistic perspective, proposing that consciousness exists independently of the body as a distinct "mind." This view suggests that while the brain may facilitate conscious thought, consciousness itself is a separate entity, perhaps even immortal. In contrast, materialist philosophers believe that consciousness is fully rooted in the brain, with no need for a "mind" outside of physical structures. This materialist view implies that consciousness is a product of biology, and when the brain ceases to function, so does consciousness.

The debate between dualism and materialism raises important questions about the essence of consciousness. For me, this exploration of consciousness as potentially separate from the body introduces a sense of wonder about what consciousness truly is. If consciousness is more than just neural activity, it suggests the possibility of experiences that transcend the physical, opening up questions about the nature of the self and the mind's potential for growth. This philosophical inquiry invites me to view consciousness not just as a function of the brain, but as a layered experience that may reach beyond the limitations of physicality.

Psychological Theories and Levels of Awareness

Psychologists contribute to the study of consciousness by exploring the various levels and types of awareness. Psychologist William James described consciousness as a "stream," a continuous flow of thoughts and sensations that make up each moment of experience. This stream of consciousness includes both the conscious mind—thoughts and sensations I am actively aware of—and the subconscious, a reservoir of experiences and memories that influence my behavior without my direct awareness. For psychologists, understanding these levels of awareness is essential to understanding how perception, memory, and emotion shape consciousness.

Sigmund Freud expanded on this idea by introducing the concept of the unconscious, a part of the mind that stores repressed memories and desires. According to Freud, the unconscious mind affects my thoughts and actions in ways I am not fully aware of, influencing everything from dreams to daily decisions. This psychological model shows that consciousness is not a single, uniform experience; it is a spectrum that includes layers of awareness, some of which operate below the surface of conscious thought. For me, this understanding of consciousness as multi-layered reveals the complexity of self-awareness, showing that my mind is shaped not only by what I know but also by what I have yet to uncover.

Consciousness as a Spectrum of Experiences

Consciousness can be understood as a spectrum that ranges from basic sensory awareness to complex, reflective thought. At one end of this spectrum are minimal forms of consciousness, such as sensory perception and basic awareness of the environment. These foundational levels of consciousness allow me to interact with the world, responding to stimuli in ways that support survival. This form of awareness is present not only in humans but also in animals, suggesting that consciousness exists on a continuum across species, each level adapting to the needs of the organism.

At the other end of the spectrum is higher-order consciousness, where self-awareness, introspection, and abstract thought come into play. This level of consciousness allows me to reflect on my experiences, question my beliefs, and imagine possibilities that go beyond immediate reality. This reflective capacity makes human consciousness unique, enabling personal growth, creativity, and the ability to ponder existential questions. For me, viewing consciousness as a spectrum reveals its versatility, showing that it is not a fixed state but an evolving experience that can expand or contract depending on awareness, mental focus, and personal development.

Consciousness and the Role of Perception

Perception is fundamental to consciousness, acting as the bridge between my mind and the external world. Each sensory experience adds depth to consciousness, turning raw data into meaningful interpretations. When I see, hear, touch, or taste something, my mind processes these sensations, creating a cohesive experience of reality. Perception not only informs me about the physical world but also influences my emotional responses, shaping how I feel and think. Without perception, consciousness would lack the richness that comes from interacting with the environment; it would be a blank slate, devoid of context.

In addition to sensory input, perception includes mental processes that interpret and filter information, allowing me to prioritize certain details while ignoring others. This selective nature of perception reveals the flexibility of consciousness, as my mind chooses what to focus on based on relevance, mood, or past experiences. For me, perception is a reminder that consciousness is not purely internal—it is shaped by my interactions with the world, creating a dynamic experience that reflects both my inner thoughts and external environment. Through perception, I experience reality in a way that is both personal and connected to the shared world.

The Emergence of Consciousness: An Ongoing Mystery

While science has made significant strides in understanding the brain, the emergence of consciousness remains a mystery. How does subjective awareness arise from biological processes? How do neurons and brain chemistry give rise to experiences, thoughts, and self-reflection? These questions drive research into consciousness, inspiring scientists and philosophers alike to explore the "hard problem" of consciousness—the question of how physical matter produces subjective experience. For now, this question remains unanswered, highlighting the complexity and depth of consciousness as a phenomenon that cannot be fully explained by current knowledge.

For me, the mystery of consciousness adds a sense of wonder to my understanding of the mind. It suggests that consciousness may have dimensions that are not yet accessible through scientific methods, opening up possibilities for further exploration and discovery. This unknown aspect of consciousness reminds me that while science can illuminate many aspects of life, there are still areas that elude understanding, inviting curiosity and a sense of humility. The emergence of consciousness is a testament to the mind's complexity, showing that awareness is a gift that I am still learning to comprehend fully.

Reflections on the Foundations of Consciousness

The foundations of consciousness encompass biological, philosophical, and psychological perspectives, each offering a unique insight into the nature of awareness. From the neural processes that generate perception to the philosophical debates about mind and body, consciousness is a multi-layered experience that defies simple explanation. For me, exploring these foundations reveals that consciousness is both a tangible phenomenon rooted in the brain and a mysterious experience that invites deeper reflection. Each perspective adds to my understanding, showing that consciousness is not just about being aware but about experiencing reality in ways that are rich, complex, and deeply meaningful.

This chapter is a reminder that consciousness is not a single, unified experience; it is a spectrum of awareness that includes everything from sensory perception to self-reflection. By embracing this spectrum, I gain a fuller understanding of my own mind, recognizing that consciousness is not static but a dynamic journey of discovery. Whether through biology, philosophy, or psychology, each perspective on consciousness brings me closer to understanding the essence of awareness, inviting me to explore the depths of the mind and the mysteries of existence.

Chapter 3: Perceptual Reality and Hallucinations

Perception shapes how I understand reality, providing a lens through which I interpret the world. However, perception is not always an accurate reflection of reality; it is influenced by sensory input, memory, emotions, and sometimes even the mind's ability to create alternate experiences. Hallucinations, for instance, are powerful examples of how perception can diverge from reality, generating vivid experiences that feel real but are not grounded in the external world. In examining perception and hallucination, I uncover the flexible, often mysterious, nature of consciousness and how my mind constructs a version of reality that is both subjective and susceptible to distortion.

Constructing Reality through Perception

Perception is a process that constructs my reality by interpreting sensory information from the environment. Each moment, my senses collect data that my brain processes, turning raw input into a coherent picture of the world. However, this picture is not purely objective; it is influenced by my experiences, beliefs, and emotions, all of which shape how I interpret sensory information. For example, when I encounter a familiar place, my memories of that location influence how I perceive it, adding layers of meaning that go beyond what my senses detect.

This constructive nature of perception reveals that reality is, to some extent, subjective. While I rely on my senses to navigate the world, my perception is filtered through a mental framework that colors how I interpret each experience. This process allows me to make sense of the world, but it also introduces biases, creating a reality that is unique to my consciousness. Perception, therefore, is not just about seeing what is; it is about interpreting, contextualizing, and assigning meaning to the sensory input I receive. For me, this constructed reality highlights the complexity of consciousness, showing that perception is a blend of objective information and subjective interpretation.

The Role of Hallucinations in Shaping Perception

Hallucinations are vivid experiences that occur in the absence of external stimuli, revealing the mind's ability to create alternate realities. During a hallucination, my mind generates sensory experiences—sights, sounds, or even sensations—that feel as real as any external event. These experiences demonstrate that perception is not always tied to the external world; it can also emerge from within, shaped by the mind's internal processes. Hallucinations provide a unique window into consciousness, showing how the brain can construct realities that, while disconnected from the physical world, are deeply convincing.

For me, hallucinations are both fascinating and humbling. They reveal the extent to which my mind can create its own version of reality, challenging my assumptions about what is real and what is imagined. When I experience a hallucination, it feels as though my mind has taken over my senses, presenting a reality that is vivid but entirely internal. This phenomenon reminds me that perception is not a straightforward reflection of the world; it is a dynamic process that can be influenced by both external and internal factors. Hallucinations, therefore, show the flexibility of perception, suggesting that consciousness is capable of creating experiences that transcend ordinary reality.

Hallucinations and the Brain's Role in Perception

The brain plays a central role in shaping perception, and hallucinations reveal the mechanisms through which the brain constructs reality. Neurotransmitters, brain regions, and neural networks work together to interpret sensory input, creating a seamless experience of the world. However, when these processes are disrupted—whether by mental illness, substance use, or neurological conditions—the brain can produce hallucinations, generating sensory experiences that do not correspond to external stimuli. These disruptions reveal the fragility of perception, showing that the mind's interpretation of reality is highly dependent on the brain's internal workings.

For example, dopamine—a neurotransmitter associated with reward and pleasure—can influence hallucinations, especially in conditions like schizophrenia. Elevated dopamine levels can cause the brain to misinterpret stimuli, leading to sensory experiences that feel real but have no basis in the external world. This connection between neurochemistry and hallucination highlights the biological foundation of perception, showing that consciousness is rooted in the brain's physical processes. For me, understanding the brain's role in perception underscores the complexity of consciousness, reminding me that what I perceive is shaped by both mental and biological factors.

CONSCIOUSNESS AND PERCEPTION

The Power of Suggestion and Perception

The power of suggestion reveals another layer of flexibility in perception, demonstrating how my expectations and beliefs can shape my experience of reality. For instance, when I anticipate hearing a sound or seeing a specific image, my mind becomes more attuned to that possibility, sometimes to the extent that I actually perceive it. This phenomenon, known as expectancy bias, shows that perception is not entirely passive; it is influenced by what I expect to see or hear. When I am highly suggestible, my perception becomes more malleable, as though my mind is open to interpreting sensory input in ways that align with my expectations.

This power of suggestion plays a significant role in experiences like placebo effects, where my belief in a treatment's effectiveness can lead to real physical or emotional changes. In these cases, perception and expectation are intertwined, creating a reality that feels genuine even if it lacks a basis in objective fact. For me, the power of suggestion is a reminder that perception is influenced not only by external stimuli but also by my mental state. When I am aware of this influence, I can approach perception with a sense of curiosity, recognizing that reality is shaped not only by what is present but also by what I believe and expect to be true.

Distinguishing Reality from Illusion

One of the challenges of perception is distinguishing reality from illusion, particularly when my senses are influenced by biases, expectations, or hallucinations. Illusions, whether optical or auditory, trick my senses into perceiving something that isn't there, creating a gap between what I see and what is real. This gap highlights the mind's tendency to fill in blanks, using patterns and assumptions to create a coherent picture of the world. While these mental shortcuts are useful for navigating everyday life, they also introduce distortions, showing that perception is not always a reliable guide to reality.

For example, optical illusions reveal the brain's reliance on patterns, as I often see shapes or colors that do not align with the physical world. These illusions remind me that perception is constructed, shaped by the brain's interpretation rather than a direct representation of reality. In moments of illusion, I am reminded of the limits of my senses, recognizing that what I perceive is filtered through a mental process that can sometimes mislead me. For me, the experience of illusions is a reminder of the fluid nature of perception, showing that reality is not always what it seems and that consciousness is capable of creating experiences that feel real but are ultimately constructed.

The Impact of Memory on Perception

Memory plays a crucial role in shaping perception, as past experiences provide context for interpreting the present. When I encounter a familiar situation, my memory of similar events influences how I perceive it, adding layers of meaning that go beyond sensory input. This influence can enhance perception, allowing me to interpret experiences with a sense of continuity, but it can also introduce biases. For example, if I have a negative memory associated with a certain place, I may perceive it as uncomfortable or unsettling even if there is no immediate reason to feel that way.

Memory can also create illusions, as the mind sometimes reconstructs past events inaccurately, leading me to perceive reality in ways that align with my recollections rather than the present moment. False memories, in particular, reveal how perception can be shaped by subjective interpretations rather than objective truth. When I rely on memory to understand the present, I am aware that my perception is influenced by past experiences, creating a reality that is unique to my personal history. For me, memory is both a guide and a filter, providing valuable context while also reminding me that perception is not entirely grounded in the present.

Reflections on Perception and Reality

Exploring the nature of perception and hallucinations reveals the fluid, complex nature of consciousness. Each layer—whether constructed reality, the power of suggestion, hallucinations, or memory—shows that perception is not a fixed reflection of the world but a dynamic process shaped by both external and internal factors. While perception allows me to navigate reality, it also highlights the limits of my understanding, reminding me that consciousness is capable of creating experiences that go beyond the tangible world.

For me, these reflections are a reminder that perception is both a gift and a limitation. It enables me to interpret the world, but it also introduces distortions that challenge my sense of what is real. By understanding the ways in which perception is shaped, I approach consciousness with curiosity, recognizing that reality is a blend of sensory input, mental interpretation, and personal experience. This awareness encourages me to remain open to

CONSCIOUSNESS AND PERCEPTION

alternative perspectives, knowing that my perception of reality is but one possible version in a vast, multifaceted universe.

Chapter 4: The Mind-Body Connection

The mind and body are often seen as separate entities, yet they are intricately connected, influencing each other in profound ways. This connection shapes perception, emotions, and physical health, revealing the interplay between mental states and bodily experiences. Through the mind-body connection, I gain insight into how physical sensations influence my thoughts and emotions and, in turn, how my mental state affects my physical experience. Reflecting on this connection offers a holistic perspective on consciousness, showing that the mind and body are not isolated but interdependent parts of a unified experience.

Physical States and Perception

Physical states such as fatigue, illness, and high energy levels directly impact my perception of reality. When I am fatigued, my senses feel duller, and my awareness becomes limited, as though my mind is operating on a lower frequency. This physical state affects my mental clarity and focus, making it difficult to engage fully with my surroundings. In contrast, when I am in optimal health, my senses feel heightened, and I am more attuned to the world. High energy creates a sense of mental sharpness that enhances my perception, allowing me to experience reality with a heightened sense of presence and engagement.

The effect of physical states on perception reveals how deeply intertwined the mind and body are. My body provides the sensory input, while my mind interprets and assigns meaning to that input. For instance, when I am unwell, even familiar environments can feel overwhelming or unsettling, as though my altered physical state has shifted my perception of reality. This experience reminds me that perception is not only a mental process but also a physical one, influenced by the body's condition and its interaction with the environment. The mind-body connection creates a feedback loop where physical sensations and mental interpretations continuously shape each other.

Emotions as Physical Experiences

Emotions are often thought of as mental states, yet they are deeply rooted in the body. When I feel joy, my body responds with a sense of lightness and energy, as though my physical state is reflecting my mental state. Conversely,

CONSCIOUSNESS AND PERCEPTION

feelings of sadness or stress are accompanied by sensations of heaviness or tension, making my body feel burdened by the weight of emotion. These physical responses to emotions demonstrate that the mind and body are not separate in experiencing feelings; they are both engaged in the process, creating an embodied emotional experience.

The physical nature of emotions reveals how the mind-body connection shapes my perception of the world. Emotions color my experiences, influencing how I interpret and respond to situations. For example, when I am happy, I view my surroundings with a sense of openness, noticing details that may go unnoticed when I am stressed. In contrast, negative emotions create a filter that narrows my focus, making me more aware of threats or challenges. These emotional states are not purely mental—they are felt in the body, creating a full sensory experience that shapes how I perceive reality. For me, this embodiment of emotions highlights the unity of mind and body, showing that consciousness is not confined to the mind but is a holistic experience.

Trauma and Its Long-Lasting Effects on Perception

Trauma is a powerful example of how deeply the mind and body are connected, as it leaves lasting imprints on both mental and physical experiences. Traumatic events create memories that are stored not only in the mind but also in the body, affecting how I respond to similar situations in the future. For example, when I encounter a situation that reminds me of a past trauma, my body reacts before my mind has fully processed the experience. My heart rate may increase, muscles tense, and breathing quickens, as though my body remembers the trauma even when I am not consciously aware of it. This physiological response to trauma demonstrates that the mind and body retain memories in ways that shape perception and behavior.

The mind-body connection in trauma reveals how past experiences influence present perception. Trauma creates a heightened state of alertness, where the body is constantly prepared for potential threats, even in safe environments. This hyper-awareness affects my perception, making me more sensitive to certain stimuli and more likely to interpret situations as dangerous. For me, understanding the impact of trauma on the mind and body highlights the lasting effects of past experiences, showing that perception is not always based on present reality but can be shaped by memories stored within the body. This connection between trauma, memory, and perception reminds me of the complexity of consciousness, where past and present merge to influence how I experience reality.

The Influence of Neurochemistry on Mood and Perception

Neurochemistry plays a significant role in the mind-body connection, influencing mood, perception, and overall mental well-being. Chemicals such as dopamine, serotonin, and cortisol affect how I feel and perceive the world, acting as messengers that shape my mental and physical states. For instance, high levels of dopamine are associated with feelings of pleasure and reward, creating a sense of motivation and focus. This chemical shift enhances my perception, making experiences feel more engaging and fulfilling. In contrast, an imbalance in neurochemistry, such as low serotonin levels, can lead to feelings of sadness or anxiety, altering my perception in ways that make the world feel less inviting.

These neurochemical shifts show that consciousness is not only shaped by mental states but also by physical processes within the brain. When my neurochemistry is balanced, I experience a sense of well-being that enhances my engagement with life. However, when there is an imbalance, my perception of reality becomes skewed, as though a filter has been placed over my consciousness. This biochemical basis for perception highlights the intricate connection between mind and body, where internal physical processes shape how I interpret and engage with the world. For me, neurochemistry is a reminder that consciousness is not solely a product of thought; it is influenced by the chemical interactions within the body that support mental states.

Mindfulness and the Power of Mind-Body Awareness

Mindfulness is a practice that strengthens the mind-body connection by encouraging awareness of both mental and physical experiences. When I practice mindfulness, I become more attuned to the sensations in my body, observing how thoughts, emotions, and physical states are interconnected. This awareness allows me to recognize patterns in my reactions, helping me understand how my body responds to different mental states. For example, when I feel anxious, I notice that my shoulders tense and my breathing becomes shallow. By observing these physical cues, I can take steps to calm my body, which in turn helps to ease my anxiety.

Through mindfulness, I gain a deeper understanding of how the mind and body influence each other. This practice empowers me to manage my reactions by paying attention to physical sensations, using the body as a tool for grounding and calming the mind. Mindfulness reveals that consciousness is not just about thinking—it is about being present with the body, engaging in an embodied experience that brings mental clarity and physical well-being. For me, mindfulness is a pathway to understanding the mind-body connection, as it shows that self-awareness involves both mental insight and physical attunement.

Imagination and the Physical Experience of Mental States

The mind-body connection extends to imagination, where mental imagery can create physical sensations. When I vividly imagine a scenario, my body responds as though I am actually experiencing it. For instance, if I imagine standing on the edge of a cliff, I may feel my heart race or my stomach tighten, even though I am physically safe. This response shows that the mind's ability to create mental images can elicit physical reactions, demonstrating the power of imagination to bridge the gap between thought and sensation.

Imagination's impact on the body reveals how deeply intertwined mental states and physical experiences are. By visualizing positive or calming scenarios, I can influence my body's stress response, creating a sense of relaxation and peace. This connection between imagination and the body is a powerful tool for managing stress and promoting well-being, as it allows me to engage in mental practices that enhance physical health. For me, the physical experience of imagination underscores the unity of mind and body, showing that consciousness is not confined to the mind but extends into the sensory experiences that shape how I feel.

Reflections on the Mind-Body Connection

The mind-body connection reveals a holistic perspective on consciousness, where mental states and physical experiences are interwoven in ways that shape perception, emotions, and health. Each influence—from physical states and emotions to neurochemistry, mindfulness, and imagination—shows that consciousness is not limited to the mind but is a unified experience that includes the body. This interconnectedness provides a deeper understanding of reality, highlighting that perception is a product of both mental interpretation and physical sensation.

For me, the mind-body connection is a reminder that consciousness is dynamic, shaped by a continuous exchange between thoughts and physical states. This awareness encourages me to cultivate practices that support both mental and physical well-being, as I recognize that caring for the body is as important as nurturing the mind. By embracing the mind-body connection, I approach life with a sense of balance and integration, appreciating the richness of consciousness as a holistic experience.

Chapter 5: Altered States of Consciousness

Altered states of consciousness, whether experienced through dreams, meditation, or psychosis, reveal unique dimensions of the mind. These states disrupt typical perception, allowing for experiences that differ significantly from ordinary waking consciousness. Altered states reveal the mind's potential for depth and flexibility, suggesting that consciousness can be molded in ways that go beyond the usual boundaries of perception. By exploring these altered states, I gain insights into how the mind constructs reality and discover possibilities for experiencing awareness in new, often profound, ways. In each altered state, I encounter different facets of reality, learning more about consciousness and its ability to transcend the ordinary.

Dreams as a Window into the Mind's Creativity

Dreams are one of the most accessible and common altered states of consciousness, providing a window into the mind's creativity and subconscious thoughts. When I dream, I experience a reality that feels as vivid and immersive as waking life, yet it is entirely constructed within my mind. Dreams allow me to explore scenarios, emotions, and perspectives that may not appear in my waking experience, revealing aspects of myself that are often hidden. In dreams, I am free from the constraints of logic and physical limitations, allowing for a fluid experience where anything feels possible.

For me, dreams offer an opportunity to explore parts of my subconscious mind, often revealing unresolved emotions, desires, or fears. When I reflect on my dreams, I notice recurring themes or symbols that seem to carry deeper meaning, as though my subconscious is communicating with me through images and stories. Dreams remind me that consciousness is not bound by waking reality; it is capable of creating worlds that, while imaginary, feel profoundly real. This creativity reveals the depth of the mind's potential, showing that perception is not limited to the external world but can also emerge from within.

Meditation and the Experience of Stillness

Meditation offers a different form of altered consciousness, one characterized by a heightened sense of stillness and presence. Unlike dreams, where the mind is active and imaginative, meditation encourages me to quiet my thoughts and focus on the present moment. In meditation, I am fully aware of each breath, sensation, and thought that arises, yet I observe them without attachment. This practice of nonjudgmental awareness creates a sense of calm that allows me to experience consciousness in its simplest form, free from the distractions of everyday life.

Through meditation, I find that my perception of time slows down, allowing me to savor each passing moment. This shift in time perception provides a unique perspective on consciousness, one that emphasizes being rather than doing. In this state of calm, I feel a deeper connection to myself and the world, as though the boundaries between my mind and my surroundings are dissolving. Meditation reveals a dimension of consciousness that is often overlooked in the rush of daily life—a state of pure awareness that is both expansive and grounding. For me, meditation is a reminder that consciousness is not only about thought and action but also about presence and connection.

Psychosis and the Fragility of Perception

Psychosis, an altered state marked by hallucinations or delusions, offers a more unsettling perspective on consciousness. Unlike dreams or meditation, where I can explore consciousness in a safe and controlled way, psychosis disrupts perception in ways that feel disorienting and, at times, frightening. During episodes of psychosis, the line between reality and imagination becomes blurred, creating a sense of confusion that challenges my understanding of what is real. This state reveals the fragility of perception, showing that consciousness is not always stable and can be subject to profound alterations that reshape how I see the world.

In experiencing psychosis, I encounter visions or thoughts that feel as real as the physical world, yet they exist only in my mind. These experiences reveal the mind's capacity to create alternate realities, suggesting that perception is not always an accurate reflection of the external world. Psychosis highlights the power of the mind to shape reality in ways that are both vivid and distorted, challenging the assumption that perception is a reliable guide to truth. For me, psychosis is a humbling reminder of the limits of perception and the complex relationship between consciousness and reality, revealing how easily the mind can construct illusions that feel deeply convincing.

The Role of Altered States in Self-Discovery

CONSCIOUSNESS AND PERCEPTION

Each altered state of consciousness provides unique opportunities for self-discovery, allowing me to explore different aspects of my identity and beliefs. In dreams, I can confront hidden fears or desires, experiencing situations that reveal parts of myself that I may not acknowledge in waking life. These dreams act as mirrors, reflecting back emotions or thoughts that reside in my subconscious, providing insight into my inner world. When I reflect on these dreams, I gain a deeper understanding of my motivations, insecurities, and aspirations, discovering aspects of myself that shape my identity in profound ways.

Meditation, on the other hand, encourages self-discovery through stillness and awareness. By quieting my mind and observing my thoughts, I become aware of the patterns and tendencies that shape my consciousness. Meditation allows me to examine my reactions, desires, and habits without judgment, creating a space for self-acceptance and growth. This practice helps me to see myself more clearly, revealing a sense of identity that is rooted in presence rather than thought. For me, meditation is a tool for self-discovery that provides clarity, helping me to align my actions with my values and deepen my connection to myself.

Even psychosis, though challenging, offers insights into self-perception. While this state is often overwhelming, it reveals the mind's capacity to shape reality in ways that are influenced by both internal and external factors. Through the distortions of psychosis, I glimpse the vulnerability of my mind and the potential for perception to create realities that differ drastically from the shared world. This experience of altered perception encourages me to reflect on the stability of my sense of self, showing that identity is not always fixed but can be altered by changes in consciousness. For me, psychosis is a reminder of the mind's complexity and the need for compassion and understanding in navigating the boundaries of reality.

The Realness of Altered States

One of the most intriguing aspects of altered states is the sense of "realness" they often bring. Whether in a dream, during meditation, or through a psychotic episode, these states feel as vivid and convincing as waking life. This realness raises questions about the nature of reality and the boundaries of consciousness, suggesting that there may be multiple layers to existence. When I am immersed in an altered state, the experiences feel authentic, challenging the assumption that only waking consciousness reflects true reality. These states remind me that consciousness is capable of creating worlds that feel as real as the physical environment, blurring the line between internal and external reality.

For example, the emotions I experience in dreams are just as intense as those I feel in waking life, even though the scenarios are imaginary. Similarly, the stillness of meditation feels profound and grounding, as though I am connecting to a deeper reality that transcends my usual awareness. In psychosis, the visions or thoughts that arise seem to have a life of their own, existing in a reality that, while subjective, feels entirely convincing. This sense of realness in altered states challenges my perception of truth, suggesting that consciousness may be more fluid and expansive than I typically realize.

The Potential of Altered States for Personal Growth

Altered states of consciousness offer valuable opportunities for personal growth, as they allow me to step outside the usual boundaries of perception and explore new dimensions of awareness. In dreams, I can experiment with different roles or scenarios, gaining insight into my reactions and preferences in ways that are free from the constraints of reality. Meditation fosters a sense of mindfulness and acceptance, helping me cultivate patience, resilience, and compassion. Even the challenges of psychosis, though difficult, teach me about the mind's complexity and the importance of self-compassion in navigating difficult experiences.

For me, altered states are more than temporary disruptions—they are opportunities to expand my understanding of consciousness and my potential for growth. Each altered state reveals a different aspect of my mind, showing me how perception can be shaped, molded, and transformed in ways that enrich my understanding of myself and the world. By embracing these altered states, I learn to approach consciousness with curiosity and openness, recognizing that each experience contributes to my journey of self-discovery and personal growth. In this way, altered states are not just deviations from the norm; they are pathways to deeper understanding and inner transformation.

Chapter 6: The Limits of Perception

Perception is a remarkable tool, allowing us to interpret and navigate the world. Yet, for all its richness, perception has limits—boundaries beyond which our senses cannot reach, biases that distort reality, and illusions that trick the mind. These limitations shape our understanding of reality, reminding us that what we perceive is only a fraction of what exists. By exploring the boundaries of perception, I gain insight into the nature of consciousness and the ways in which my mind constructs a version of reality that, while functional, may not fully capture the truth.

Cognitive Biases and the Distortion of Reality

One of the most pervasive limitations of perception is cognitive bias, which shapes how I interpret information based on preexisting beliefs and experiences. Biases like confirmation bias, for instance, lead me to seek out information that aligns with what I already believe, reinforcing my perspective and filtering out alternative viewpoints. This selective perception can be both comforting and limiting, creating a version of reality that reflects my biases more than objective truth. When I'm aware of my biases, I can challenge them, but they often operate subtly, influencing my perception without my conscious awareness.

Cognitive biases also affect how I see myself and others. For example, the halo effect causes me to judge people based on one positive or negative trait, overlooking the complexity of their character. This bias simplifies my perception, making it easier to categorize people but preventing me from seeing them fully. Recognizing these biases is a humbling reminder that perception is not infallible; it is shaped by mental shortcuts that, while helpful in navigating daily life, distort the richness of reality. For me, understanding cognitive biases is crucial to developing a more nuanced and compassionate view of others, as it helps me to question my initial judgments and seek a deeper understanding.

Visual Illusions and the Fragility of Perception

Visual illusions reveal just how fragile perception can be, highlighting the ways in which our senses can be deceived. Illusions such as the Müller-Lyer illusion, where lines of equal length appear different due to the orientation of arrows at their ends, demonstrate that perception is not always aligned with objective reality. These illusions trick the mind into seeing things that aren't there, reminding me that perception is as much about interpretation as it is about sensation. Each illusion underscores the limits of my visual system, showing that my mind constructs reality based on patterns and expectations rather than purely on sensory input.

For me, visual illusions are fascinating because they reveal the brain's tendency to fill in gaps and make assumptions. When I encounter an illusion, I'm reminded of how perception relies on shortcuts—cognitive processes that allow me to quickly interpret my surroundings but that can also lead to errors. This tendency to rely on mental shortcuts means that perception is not purely objective; it is shaped by the brain's need to make sense of limited information in a fast and efficient way. Visual illusions thus reveal the constructed nature of reality, highlighting the ways in which perception is influenced by both sensory data and mental expectations.

The Role of Memory in Shaping Perception

Memory plays a significant role in perception, shaping how I interpret the present based on past experiences. Each time I encounter a familiar situation, my memory recalls previous experiences, allowing me to navigate the present with context. However, memory is not always accurate—it is prone to distortion, forgetfulness, and even false memories. When my perception is influenced by inaccurate memories, I may interpret situations in ways that don't fully align with reality. This interaction between memory and perception creates a subjective view of the world, where my understanding of the present is colored by the imperfect recollection of the past.

False memories, in particular, reveal the malleability of perception. When I remember an event inaccurately, that memory can shape my beliefs and reactions as though it were true. These false memories act as filters, influencing how I perceive myself and others based on events that may not have actually happened. This potential for distortion highlights a fundamental limit of perception: it is always influenced by the mind's interpretation of past experiences. For me, memory serves as both a guide and a bias, providing valuable context but also shaping perception in ways that are not always accurate.

The Boundary of Sensory Perception

CONSCIOUSNESS AND PERCEPTION

Human perception is limited to the range of our senses—sight, hearing, taste, smell, and touch. However, these senses can only detect a fraction of the information available in the environment. For instance, human vision is limited to the visible spectrum, leaving us unable to see ultraviolet or infrared light. Similarly, our hearing is confined to a specific frequency range, making us deaf to sounds that fall outside of that range. These sensory limitations mean that there is much about reality that remains beyond our reach, inaccessible through our natural perception.

Reflecting on these sensory boundaries reminds me that my perception of reality is inherently limited. There are dimensions of existence—colors, sounds, and energies—that I cannot experience directly, yet they are no less real. The existence of these imperceptible aspects of reality humbles me, reminding me that my perception is only one small window into a vast, multifaceted universe. While I can extend my senses through technology, such as infrared cameras or ultrasound devices, these tools only offer indirect glimpses of the broader spectrum of existence. For me, the limits of sensory perception highlight the partial nature of human experience, emphasizing that there is always more to reality than meets the eye.

The Influence of Cultural and Societal Limits on Perception

Culture and society also shape the boundaries of perception, influencing what I pay attention to and how I interpret it. Cultural norms dictate certain ways of seeing the world, creating a framework within which perception operates. For example, in cultures that value individualism, people may focus more on personal achievements and autonomy, whereas in collectivist societies, the emphasis may be on relationships and community. These cultural perspectives shape how I perceive social interactions, success, and even self-worth, creating a lens through which I interpret my experiences.

Societal expectations, such as gender roles and social hierarchies, further shape my perception by defining what is considered "normal" or "acceptable." These influences often operate subconsciously, affecting my perception in ways I might not immediately recognize. When I reflect on these cultural and societal influences, I see that perception is not solely an individual experience; it is shaped by the collective beliefs and values of the society in which I live. For me, acknowledging these influences is essential to understanding my perception more fully, as it allows me to question assumptions and explore perspectives that may lie outside my cultural framework.

Imagination and the Boundaries of Perception

Imagination allows me to transcend the limits of perception, envisioning realities that are not immediately accessible to the senses. Through imagination, I can explore worlds beyond my direct experience, creating mental landscapes that challenge the boundaries of what is possible. Imagination enables me to "see" things that aren't physically present, offering a form of perception that is rooted in creativity rather than sensory input. This mental flexibility expands my understanding of reality, allowing me to engage with possibilities that are unconstrained by the limits of my senses.

However, imagination can also blur the line between reality and fantasy, introducing a new kind of perceptual limit. When I imagine something vividly, it can feel real, influencing my emotions and reactions as though it were part of my physical environment. This blending of imagination and perception reveals a unique boundary, where the mind creates experiences that, while not based in external reality, still impact my internal world. For me, imagination represents both a liberation from sensory limits and a reminder that perception is a subjective experience, one that is shaped as much by what I imagine as by what I actually perceive.

Reflections on the Limits of Perception

Exploring the limits of perception reveals the boundaries within which consciousness operates. Cognitive biases, visual illusions, sensory limitations, cultural influences, and imagination all shape my perception, creating a version of reality that is both functional and limited. While perception allows me to navigate the world effectively, it is also a reminder that my experience is inherently subjective, shaped by factors that extend beyond objective reality. Each limitation offers insight into the nature of consciousness, showing that while perception connects me to the world, it also restricts me to a partial understanding.

For me, these limits are not shortcomings but opportunities for growth. By recognizing the boundaries of perception, I become more open to alternative perspectives, aware that there is always more to reality than what I can see, hear, or understand. This awareness encourages me to question my assumptions, seek new experiences, and remain curious about the unknown. In embracing the

CONSCIOUSNESS AND PERCEPTION

limits of perception, I find a humility that enriches my understanding of the world, reminding me that consciousness is an ever-evolving journey, one that will always have new depths to explore.

Chapter 7: The Self and the Other

Our understanding of ourselves is shaped not only by personal experiences but also by our interactions with others. Consciousness doesn't exist in isolation; it is a product of social engagement, constantly evolving through connections and contrasts with other people. Through the lens of self and other, I learn to define my identity, values, and sense of purpose. This dynamic relationship with others provides a mirror that reflects aspects of myself I may not notice alone, revealing new layers of identity that are shaped and reshaped in every interaction. In reflecting on how consciousness navigates the space between self and other, I find that my sense of identity becomes both grounded and enriched by these social encounters.

Interpersonal Perception and the Influence of Others

The way I see myself is strongly influenced by how others perceive me, whether through family, friends, or broader social circles. When I interact with others, I receive feedback—both verbal and nonverbal—that informs my self-perception. This feedback creates a continuous loop, where my understanding of myself is mirrored by the impressions of those around me. Each encounter adds a new layer to my self-concept, helping me see myself in ways I might not otherwise consider. Through these interactions, I come to understand not only how others view me but also how I wish to present myself to the world.

In social settings, group dynamics shape my self-perception by highlighting traits I might overlook when alone. For instance, the qualities I emphasize with friends differ from those I reveal to family or colleagues. This variability in how I present myself suggests that identity is flexible, adjusting to different social contexts. However, this adaptability doesn't mean that I lose my core self; rather, it shows that identity is complex, with multiple facets that emerge depending on the social situation. For me, this fluidity is a reminder that the self is not static—it is a reflection of both personal values and the social contexts in which those values are expressed.

Balancing Individuality and Belonging

The tension between individuality and belonging is a recurring theme in my relationship with others. While I value the sense of connection that comes with belonging to a group, I am also mindful of the importance of maintaining my autonomy. Belonging provides a sense of identity that is rooted in shared beliefs and values, yet this connection can sometimes feel constraining if it limits my self-expression. I find myself negotiating this balance, seeking a space where I can engage with others without losing sight of who I am. This process of balancing individuality and belonging is essential to my understanding of self and other, as it allows me to connect authentically while preserving my unique perspective.

There are times when I feel the need to distance myself from group identity to explore my own beliefs and values. This period of isolation provides a necessary contrast to social interaction, allowing me to reflect on who I am outside of societal expectations. In these moments, I reconnect with my core identity, affirming the qualities and values that define me independently of others. This oscillation between connection and solitude reveals the dynamic nature of identity, where I find balance by engaging with others while also creating space for introspection and self-discovery.

Empathy and the Expansion of Perspective

Empathy is one of the most transformative aspects of my relationship with others. By allowing me to see situations from another person's perspective, empathy expands my understanding of the world, bridging the gap between self and other. When I practice empathy, I step outside of my own viewpoint, experiencing a moment of shared consciousness that deepens my connection to others. This act of empathy not only enhances my understanding of others but also reveals parts of myself that I may not have fully explored. Through empathy, I gain insight into the emotional landscapes of others, enriching my perception of the world.

Empathy also challenges me to confront my own biases, as it encourages me to approach situations with an open mind. When I see someone else's struggles or joys, I am reminded that each individual has a unique story, shaped by experiences that are both similar to and different from my own. This awareness fosters a sense of humility, reminding me that my perspective is just one of many. In this way, empathy serves as a bridge between self and other, inviting me to connect with people on a deeper level and expanding my consciousness beyond personal boundaries.

Imagined Figures and Projected Identities

In addition to real-life interactions, my sense of self is shaped by imagined figures and projected identities. These imagined personas allow me to explore different aspects of myself, creating a space where I can experiment with identity in ways that might not be possible in everyday life. For example, by embodying certain traits or values in these imagined figures, I can explore ideals that inspire me or confront fears that challenge me. These personas serve as extensions of my consciousness, providing insight into the qualities I aspire to develop or the vulnerabilities I seek to understand.

Projected identities also play a role in how I interact with others, as they allow me to present different facets of myself depending on the social context. When I engage with people online, for instance, I may adopt a version of myself that emphasizes creativity or curiosity. These projected identities are not fabrications but rather selective expressions of who I am, shaped by the unique dynamics of each interaction. For me, this ability to adapt and present different aspects of myself highlights the flexibility of identity, showing that the self is not confined to a single narrative but is instead a mosaic of traits, experiences, and aspirations.

The Self and Collective Consciousness

My understanding of self is also influenced by collective consciousness, the shared beliefs and values that connect me to a larger community. This collective identity provides a framework through which I can explore my role within society, allowing me to see myself as part of a greater whole. In moments of connection with others, I experience a sense of unity that transcends individual identity, as though my consciousness is part of a larger, interconnected web of thoughts, emotions, and experiences. This collective consciousness reminds me that I am not alone in my journey; I am part of a shared human experience that is both unique and universal.

Collective consciousness also shapes my sense of purpose, as it reminds me of the impact my actions can have on others. When I contribute to a group or engage in activities that align with shared values, I feel a sense of fulfillment that goes beyond personal satisfaction. This sense of belonging to a collective identity adds depth to my individual identity, allowing me to see myself not just as an isolated self but as a contributor to a larger narrative. For me, the interplay between self and collective consciousness is a reminder that identity is not only personal—it is also communal, reflecting the values and beliefs of the society in which I live.

Reflections on Self and Other

The relationship between self and other is a dynamic interplay that shapes my consciousness, influencing how I see myself and how I connect with the world. Each interaction adds a new layer to my understanding of identity, revealing traits that emerge only in relation to others. Through empathy, I am able to connect deeply, experiencing a shared consciousness that expands my perspective. In moments of solitude, I reconnect with my individuality, affirming the qualities that define me independently of social influences. This continuous dialogue between self and other is what shapes my sense of self, creating a balance between autonomy and connection.

For me, the exploration of self and other is a journey of growth and discovery. Each encounter challenges me to redefine my values, examine my beliefs, and embrace the complexity of identity. Whether through the reflections of real-life interactions or the imagined figures that inhabit my mind, I find that my sense of self is constantly evolving, enriched by the diversity of perspectives I encounter. This chapter reminds me that identity is not a fixed entity; it is a fluid, multifaceted experience, shaped by the interplay of personal values, social connections, and the ever-expanding boundaries of consciousness.

Chapter 8: Memory and Identity

Memory is a foundation of personal identity, connecting past experiences with present understanding and future aspirations. It serves as a repository of knowledge, emotions, and insights that shapes who I am and how I perceive myself over time. Memory not only records events but also imbues them with meaning, allowing me to create a coherent narrative of my life. As I reflect on the role of memory, I recognize its powerful influence on my sense of self, my perception of reality, and the stability of my identity. Memory defines the continuity of my experiences, linking my past to the present in a way that shapes my understanding of what it means to be "me."

Memory as the Anchor of Identity

Memory acts as an anchor for my identity, preserving the essential moments and experiences that define who I am. Each memory serves as a building block, constructing a self that is both consistent and adaptable. When I recall formative experiences, they offer a sense of stability, grounding my sense of self in a timeline that spans across different stages of life. This accumulation of memories provides me with a sense of continuity, connecting who I was with who I am today. Without memory, identity would be fragmented, lacking the cohesion that comes from understanding my personal history.

In many ways, memory allows me to recognize myself through time, preserving a core identity that remains intact despite the inevitable changes that come with growth. It is through memory that I am able to revisit my values, my beliefs, and my goals, reaffirming my sense of self. When I recall significant moments, they reaffirm the traits and qualities that define me, reminding me of the journey that has shaped my character. Memory, therefore, acts as both a record and a guide, allowing me to see myself in a continuous light while embracing the changes that come with each new experience.

Memory's Role in Shaping Perception

Memory doesn't just preserve past events—it actively shapes how I perceive the present. Past experiences color my interpretation of current situations, providing context that influences how I respond. For example, when I encounter a familiar setting, my memories of that place infuse the present moment with a sense of nostalgia or familiarity. These memories add layers to my perception, making each experience richer and more complex. I find that memory serves as a lens through which I view the world, connecting past emotions and insights with the present in a way that creates a fuller understanding of reality.

This influence of memory on perception can be both a gift and a limitation. While memory provides depth, allowing me to interpret experiences with a sense of continuity, it can also introduce biases. When I rely too heavily on past experiences, I may miss new aspects of the present, seeing events through a preexisting framework that limits my openness to change. This dual role of memory—as both an enhancer and a filter—shows how it shapes my understanding of reality, infusing each moment with echoes of the past. Memory, therefore, creates a bridge between past and present, but it is a bridge that must be crossed with awareness to avoid distorting the new with the familiar.

The Complexity of False Memories

False memories introduce an intriguing complexity to the role of memory in identity. These are memories that feel real but do not accurately reflect actual events. False memories remind me of the malleability of memory and the mind's capacity to create realities that may not be rooted in fact. I experience both positive and negative emotions when I think about the idea of false memories. On one hand, they allow me to reinterpret adversity, turning past challenges into narratives of resilience. On the other, false memories can lead to a sense of conceit, where I view my experiences through a lens that might not fully reflect the truth.

The existence of false memories suggests that memory is not simply a record but a creative process. My mind reconstructs experiences based on emotions, beliefs, and biases, sometimes filling gaps with imagined details that feel just as real as actual events. This reconstructive nature of memory highlights the fluidity of identity; if my memories are not entirely accurate, then my sense of self is also, to some extent, a construct shaped by both truth and imagination. For me, false memories reveal the delicate balance between reality and perception, reminding me that identity is as much about interpretation as it is about fact.

Amnesia and Hyperthymesia: Memory Extremes and Their Impact on Identity

Amnesia and hyperthymesia represent extremes of memory, each posing unique challenges to identity. Amnesia, or memory loss, disrupts the continuity of self by removing essential parts of one's history. Without access to past experiences, it becomes difficult to maintain a cohesive identity, as memory provides the context necessary for self-reflection and growth. In cases of severe amnesia, individuals may feel as though they are disconnected from who they once were, struggling to piece together an identity in the absence of personal history. Amnesia reveals how deeply memory is tied to identity, showing that a loss of memory can lead to a disorienting sense of self.

Hyperthymesia, the ability to recall vast amounts of life events in extreme detail, creates the opposite challenge. While the retention of memories might seem advantageous, hyperthymesia can lead to an overwhelming sense of self, as individuals with this condition are constantly aware of past experiences. This constant recall makes it difficult to separate the present from the past, creating a fragmented sense of identity where each moment is imbued with an almost intrusive level of detail. Both amnesia and hyperthymesia highlight the importance of a balanced memory—one that preserves enough to provide continuity but allows for forgetting, enabling me to move forward without being weighed down by excessive recollection.

The Role of Memory in Present and Future Perception

Memory does more than shape my understanding of the past; it also guides my perception of the present and influences how I approach the future. When I draw on past experiences, I use memory as a tool for interpreting current events, allowing me to navigate life with the wisdom gained from previous challenges. Each memory serves as a reference point, reminding me of past lessons and helping me make informed decisions. This forward-looking aspect of memory gives me a sense of agency, as I am able to use my experiences to shape my future, creating a continuity that bridges past, present, and future.

In this way, memory becomes a tool for self-improvement, offering insights that inform my growth. By reflecting on past experiences, I can identify patterns in my behavior, recognize areas for improvement, and set goals that align with my evolving sense of self. Memory, therefore, is not a static record but a dynamic resource that helps me refine my identity over time. I am reminded that each memory, whether positive or negative, contributes to my understanding of myself and my potential, shaping a future that is deeply rooted in the wisdom of past experiences.

Memory and the Collective Identity

Memory extends beyond personal identity, contributing to a sense of collective consciousness. Cultural and societal memories—such as shared traditions, historical events, and family stories—provide a framework that connects me to a larger narrative. These collective memories enrich my understanding of the world, allowing me to see myself as part of a continuum that includes not only personal experiences but also the shared history of those around me. This collective identity gives depth to my individual identity, reminding me that I am part of a broader human experience.

When I participate in rituals, celebrations, or family traditions, I engage with memories that belong not only to me but to the collective consciousness of my culture and community. These shared memories create a sense of belonging, connecting me to others through a common narrative that transcends individual experience. For me, collective memory is a powerful reminder that identity is not formed in isolation; it is shaped by the memories and experiences of those who came before me, adding layers to my personal narrative and grounding my sense of self in a shared history.

Chapter 9: The Perception of Time

Time perception is an essential aspect of consciousness, changing with emotions, experiences, and mental states. It's fluid, not fixed—an experience that shifts based on my awareness and focus. Time can feel fast and fleeting during moments of joy or engagement, yet unbearably slow when I'm bored or stressed. Reflecting on time perception reveals that it is influenced not only by internal factors, like emotions and attention, but also by external factors, such as cultural and societal beliefs. In examining how I experience time, I uncover a deeper understanding of consciousness and how my mind interacts with the flow of life.

Engaged vs. Waiting: The Elasticity of Time Perception

One of the most striking aspects of time perception is how drastically it changes based on my level of engagement. When I am fully immersed in an activity, time seems to speed up. Minutes or even hours can pass without my noticing, as though I've become lost in the flow of the moment. This sensation often occurs when I'm engaged in something enjoyable or intellectually stimulating, where my attention is so absorbed that I barely register the passing of time. This experience suggests that engagement brings a certain timeless quality, allowing me to experience the present without a constant awareness of each ticking second.

In contrast, time slows to a crawl when I am waiting or feeling idle. In these moments, each second feels drawn out, as if time itself has become more substantial and weighty. This shift in perception reveals how strongly time is tied to my mental state. When I am engaged, my awareness of time dissolves; when I am bored or anxious, time becomes a palpable presence, stretching out endlessly. These contrasting experiences highlight the elasticity of time perception, showing that it is shaped by my level of engagement and focus.

The Influence of External vs. Internal Factors

Time perception is influenced by a combination of internal and external factors. I find that my mood and focus are key metrics that shape how I experience time, though external circumstances also play a significant role. When I'm in a stimulating environment, time seems to move faster, while a monotonous setting often makes it feel slower. This balance between internal and external factors suggests that time perception is not fixed but is continually molded by both my state of mind and my surroundings. In this sense, time becomes a reflection of my consciousness, adapting to the blend of internal and external stimuli.

Being constantly connected through technology adds another layer of complexity to my experience of time. In the digital age, moments are filled with continuous notifications, messages, and updates, creating a fragmented experience where my attention is frequently pulled in different directions. This perpetual connectivity accelerates my perception of time, as each digital interaction compresses my awareness into shorter, more focused bursts. For me, the pace of digital engagement alters my sense of time, making it feel faster yet less substantial. In a way, technology creates a dual reality—a fast-paced digital world alongside the slower, physical one.

Emotions as a Guide to Time Perception

Emotions are powerful guides to how I perceive time. Happiness has a unique way of transcending time, creating moments that feel almost timeless. When I'm experiencing joy or excitement, time seems to lose its usual structure, as if I am momentarily released from its bounds. These positive emotions create an expansive sense of time, allowing me to immerse myself fully in the present without the usual awareness of passing moments. Happiness accelerates my perception, making time feel light and fleeting, adding a sense of brightness to each experience.

Conversely, stress and sadness have a grounding effect on my perception of time, making it feel heavier and more prolonged. When I am anxious or overwhelmed, time becomes more defined, each moment stretching out as though anchored in place. I associate negative emotions with a slower time perception, as if they tether me to the present in a way that makes it difficult to escape. This duality of emotions—joy creating a lightness in time, and stress creating a heaviness—reveals the intricate relationship between mental state and time perception, showing how emotions serve as filters that either condense or expand my sense of temporal flow.

Memory and the Condensation of Time

Memory plays a unique role in time perception by condensing my experiences into shorter, more manageable segments. When I reflect on the past, I find that time feels compressed; entire days, months, or even years can be condensed into specific moments or feelings. This compression makes it difficult to replay an entire day's worth of memories without feeling that I've lost time in the present. It's as if memories are snapshots that capture the essence of an experience but lack the full stretch of time that accompanied the original moment. For me, this condensed nature of memory is a reminder of time's fleeting quality, reinforcing the idea that while we can revisit the past, we can never fully relive it.

Memory not only compresses time but also shapes how I perceive its passage. Reflecting on past experiences often slows down my perception of the present, as if the act of remembering anchors me momentarily outside the usual flow of time. This reflective state brings a sense of nostalgia, where I linger over memories, savoring the feeling of past moments even as I'm aware that they are gone. This interplay between memory and time perception is a bittersweet reminder of the impermanence of experiences, showing how memories can bridge the past and present but only in fragmented, condensed forms.

Time in Altered States: Dreams and Meditation

Altered states of consciousness, such as dreams and meditation, offer unique perspectives on time perception. In dreams, time feels condensed, allowing me to experience events that would normally take hours in a matter of minutes. This compression of time in dreams creates a surreal quality, where entire narratives can unfold in a short span, leaving me with the impression of having lived through a complete experience. Dreams reveal the mind's capacity to manipulate time, showing that perception is not always tied to reality and that time can be experienced in fluid, malleable ways.

Meditation, on the other hand, slows down my sense of time, allowing each moment to stretch out in a calming, measured way. Unlike dreams, where time feels condensed, meditation creates an environment of stillness, where I am fully present with each passing second. This slow pace gives me a heightened awareness of the present, making time feel expansive and spacious. For me, meditation offers a therapeutic encounter with time, revealing a sense of calm that contrasts sharply with the hurried pace of daily life. Through meditation, I experience time not as a linear flow but as a series of unfolding moments, each one bringing a sense of clarity and peace.

Dreams and meditation remind me of the flexibility of time perception, showing that it can be molded and shaped by the state of consciousness I bring into each experience. These altered states highlight the mind's power to transcend usual temporal boundaries, suggesting that time is as much a product of awareness as it is a fixed reality. For me, these experiences reveal a depth to time perception that goes beyond the everyday, offering glimpses into the possibility of time as a fluid, adaptable dimension.

Cultural and Societal Influences on Time Perception

Cultural and societal beliefs also shape how I perceive time, adding another layer to its fluid nature. In some cultures, time is seen as a linear progression, with an emphasis on productivity and efficiency. In others, time is cyclical, focusing more on the present moment and the natural flow of life. These cultural perspectives influence my own view of time, as I find myself torn between the urgency of linear time and the calm acceptance of cyclical time. The societal emphasis on productivity often makes me feel that time is a resource to be managed, while more reflective cultural practices remind me of the importance of presence.

In a broader societal context, events and trends can shift collective time perception, affecting how entire communities experience the passage of time. Major societal events, such as historical milestones or global crises, create a sense of shared time, where individual experiences merge with the collective memory. For me, these societal influences reveal how time perception is not only personal but also communal, shaped by shared narratives that bring people together across moments in history.

Chapter 10: Collective Consciousness and Social Identity

Collective consciousness connects individuals through shared beliefs, values, and cultural narratives, creating a sense of unity across social groups. It influences how we see ourselves, shaping personal and social identities in ways that impact every aspect of life. For me, collective consciousness is not just a backdrop—it's an active influence that defines how I perceive myself and others. Whether in spiritual settings, social groups, or even online communities, the collective mind has a profound effect on identity and perception, blending personal beliefs with shared values to form a cohesive sense of self within a larger context.

Understanding Collective Consciousness

I think of collective consciousness as an organized event—a sequence of beliefs and values that actively shape individuals rather than passively existing in the background. It's a force that connects people through shared narratives, whether in spiritual gatherings, social institutions, or cultural traditions. In my experiences within spiritual settings, such as church, collective consciousness has shaped my understanding of culture and the nature of human intelligence. Each gathering reminds me that personal beliefs are rarely isolated; they are part of a larger network of shared experiences that influence both individual and collective identity.

Societal events and major trends often act as catalysts, shifting collective consciousness and shaping how I see the world. I've noticed that significant social changes create ripple effects, influencing not only the beliefs of society at large but also my personal worldview. Whether it's through the rise of a new movement, the impact of a cultural moment, or even technological changes, these shifts in collective consciousness are reminders that our beliefs are interconnected. I find myself adapting my perspective in response to these changes, recognizing the fluid nature of collective identity and the role it plays in shaping my sense of self.

The Role of Groups in Shaping Identity

Group dynamics profoundly shape how I see myself, providing a mirror that reflects back my strengths, weaknesses, and values. Whether it's through family, friendships, or larger social groups, the influence of these connections on self-perception is undeniable. Certain groups—such as Christianity, Satanism, and even cultural identities like that of the United States—impact my identity in unique ways. For me, these groups represent what I consider "cool"—a term I associate with a form of intelligence that brings sophistication to moral character. These groups offer both a sense of belonging and a framework for evaluating my own beliefs, blending personal identity with shared values.

Navigating social identity can be complex, especially when I consider my tendency to live in isolation and develop unique personas and characters. In my solitude, I explore dystopian themes while also nurturing a utopian outlook. This individual journey provides a counterbalance to group identity, allowing me to cultivate a sense of self that exists independently of collective beliefs. I value the freedom to explore self-identity outside conventional norms, finding meaning in the contrast between belonging and individuality. In-group versus out-group dynamics often highlight this contrast—where in-group settings allow for deeper, personal conversations, out-group interactions tend to remain surface-level, shaped more by individual perspectives.

Being part of a group also reveals the tension between belonging and individuality. While I appreciate the sense of unity that comes with group identity, I sometimes feel that conformity can limit self-expression. Social identity, in my view, is flexible to an extent, but belonging to a group can sometimes overshadow individual traits, encouraging alignment with collective norms. This balance between unity and autonomy is an ongoing negotiation, where I strive to maintain my individuality while still engaging meaningfully with the values of the groups I associate with.

Cultural Narratives and Personal Perception

Cultural narratives play a powerful role in shaping my perception of myself and the world. At times, I find cultural beliefs both oppressive and transcendently liberating. For instance, the cultural narrative of God resonates deeply with me, influencing my worldview in complex ways. God represents a figure created by humanity yet revered with gratitude and respect, embodying both power and humility. This narrative has helped me reflect on my own values, encouraging me to consider how cultural beliefs shape identity in ways that go beyond the individual. For me, culture serves as a guide—a source of wisdom that informs my perception, while also challenging me to question and refine my beliefs.

I once tried to separate myself from the world for educational purposes, immersing myself in isolation to explore self-identity outside societal norms. This solitude led to profound insights but also introduced mental stigma, a reminder of the challenges that come with distancing oneself from cultural frameworks. In isolation, I unraveled truths about the self, yet I felt a sense of coldness and loneliness without the presence of culture and others to share my thoughts, emotions, and experiences with. These reflections revealed to me the importance of shared narratives and the warmth they bring to personal identity, emphasizing the role of culture in creating a well-rounded sense of self.

Globalization adds another layer of complexity to cultural identity, blending diverse narratives and reshaping collective beliefs on a global scale. I view globalization as a kind of attrition on the self, where external influences continuously shape both historical and personal narratives. This phenomenon strengthens my sense of self by fostering resilience and wisdom, yet it can also weaken identity when entangled with oppressive forces. For me, globalization represents both a challenge and an opportunity—a reminder that cultural identity is dynamic, adapting to the interplay of local and global influences.

Social Media and Collective Consciousness

Social media is a modern extension of collective consciousness, connecting people across the globe and creating new forms of community. I see social media as a platform for acceptance, offering space for empathy and compassion but also highlighting a sense of isolation due to the vast number of people I could never fully connect with. Social media provides a unique environment for exploring perspectives and sharing ideas, yet it often lacks the grounding reality of in-person interactions. This virtual space offers both connectivity and distance, challenging my sense of belonging and authenticity in a digital age.

When I created my first alias, I used it as a way to engage with the world socially, bringing a sense of mystery and authenticity to my interactions. This online persona became a fun, engaging extension of myself, embodying elements of my identity that I explored offline. However, I find the opposite effect when meeting notable social media figures in person—the individuality that exists online can sometimes feel elusive in real life, revealing the gap between digital and physical identities. This contrast highlights the complexity of identity in the digital age, where online interactions offer a blend of self-expression and distance from authentic experience.

Social media algorithms also play a unique role in shaping collective consciousness, guiding users toward content that reinforces certain views. While I appreciate that algorithms help users find their niche, I'm also reminded of a deeper principle: the pursuit of justice should transcend systems and institutions. This perspective encourages me to approach social media critically, recognizing both its potential for community building and the echo chambers it can create. For me, social media is a space of possibility, where connectivity must be balanced with awareness of its limitations.

Balancing Belonging and Autonomy in Collective Identity

Navigating collective consciousness and social identity is an ongoing balance between belonging and autonomy. Each group I engage with offers a sense of unity, but I'm mindful of the need to retain my individuality. Through cultural narratives, social media, and even globalization, I'm continuously shaping my sense of self, integrating shared beliefs with personal insights. The collective mind influences me in ways that are both profound and challenging, allowing me to see myself as part of a larger whole while also reminding me of the importance of independent thought.

In exploring collective consciousness, I find that social identity is both a source of connection and a framework for self-reflection. Belonging provides a foundation for understanding my values, while individuality allows me to interpret those values in ways that feel true to myself. This chapter reveals the complex dance between personal identity and collective influence, showing how each aspect of my self-concept is enriched, challenged, and ultimately defined within the larger context of shared human experience.

Chapter 11: Emotions and Perception

Emotions are intrinsic to how I perceive and understand the world. They influence my sensory experience, shape my reactions, and guide how I interpret reality. Emotions serve as filters, enhancing or distorting perception based on my mental state. Whether positive or negative, emotions provide a unique lens that continuously colors my view of myself and others. Reflecting on the role of emotions reveals how they bring depth to every experience, creating layers of meaning that go beyond simple observation.

Emotions as Filters for Perception

In my experience, emotions like joy, anger, or sadness have a profound impact on my perception. They don't just affect my mood; they shape my thought patterns and responses, serving as lenses through which I view the world. Emotions act as constant filters, giving each moment a particular tone or hue that shapes my overall experience. This influence is natural—emotions create a frame of reference, allowing me to interpret and respond to stimuli in ways that reflect my inner state. I find that emotions bring both clarity and bias, providing insight while also limiting how I see certain situations.

For instance, when I'm experiencing joy, my sensory awareness seems to heighten. I notice details that I might otherwise overlook, savoring each moment with a sense of vibrancy. On the other hand, during periods of anger or sadness, my perception narrows, focusing on specific details while excluding others. It's as though each emotion carries a particular focus, directing my attention to certain aspects of my environment and shaping how I respond. This dynamic nature of emotions reveals how perception is never neutral—it's always tinged by the emotions I bring into each moment.

Positive vs. Negative Emotional States

Positive emotions, such as happiness and excitement, foster a constructive psyche that influences perception in a beneficial way. When I feel joyful, I approach life with openness, ready to engage with the world and appreciate its beauty. Positive emotions not only lift my mood but also broaden my outlook, creating a sense of expansiveness that allows me to experience each moment fully. In these states, I find myself more aware of the small details, noticing nuances in my surroundings that enhance my sense of connection and wonder.

CONSCIOUSNESS AND PERCEPTION

Negative emotions, however, cast a different shade on my perception. Sadness, frustration, or anger can narrow my focus, sometimes causing me to withdraw from my surroundings. In these moments, my perspective contracts, and I become more introspective, often focusing on internal thoughts rather than external stimuli. Negative emotions tend to cast a shadow over my experience, limiting my ability to see beyond the immediate moment and sometimes distorting my view of reality. For me, these contrasting effects highlight the power emotions have over my perception, as if each emotion brings with it a unique reality shaped by its own mood and energy.

I find that certain emotions heighten my attention to detail, while others encourage me to detach. For example, feelings of excitement or curiosity drive me to observe more closely, taking in my surroundings with a keen eye. Conversely, when I'm overwhelmed or fatigued, I tend to overlook the details, focusing instead on larger patterns or general impressions. This balance between engagement and detachment reflects the way emotions guide my focus, influencing how deeply or superficially I engage with the world around me.

Empathy and the Perception of Others

Empathy, as an emotional state, transforms how I perceive others by allowing me to see them with understanding and compassion. When I approach situations with empathy, I'm more open to seeing people in a positive light, acknowledging their unique perspectives and emotions. Empathy enhances my ability to connect with others on a meaningful level, providing insights that I might miss otherwise. This emotional resonance allows me to go beyond my own experiences, stepping into someone else's reality to better understand their challenges and joys.

One particular moment stands out to me—a time when empathy enabled me to shift my perspective and make a better decision. In that instance, seeing the situation through someone else's eyes gave me clarity, helping me navigate a complex problem with increased intelligence. This experience reminded me of the power of empathy, not only to foster connection but also to improve my ability to respond thoughtfully. When I approach others with empathy, I feel my perception broadening, allowing me to see beyond my initial judgments and engage with a fuller understanding of the person before me.

Empathy doesn't just influence how I see others; it also shapes my sense of self. When I am empathetic, I feel a stronger connection to my own values of kindness, patience, and understanding. This alignment between self and action brings a sense of fulfillment, reinforcing the importance of emotional attunement in my perception of others. Through empathy, I learn to view people not as isolated entities but as individuals whose experiences reflect aspects of my own, reminding me of our shared humanity.

Emotional Resilience and Managing Perception

Emotional resilience plays a pivotal role in shaping how I handle challenges and setbacks. It provides a foundation that allows me to approach difficulties with calm and perspective, even when emotions run high. For me, resilience is not about suppressing emotions but about managing them in a way that supports clarity and balance. This strength acts as a buffer, helping me maintain a stable perspective and respond thoughtfully, even when faced with obstacles.

When I regulate my emotions, I notice a shift in how I perceive the world. By choosing to manage my reactions rather than letting them control me, I create an environment of empathy and compassion. This regulation allows me to approach situations with a welcoming attitude, making space for understanding rather than judgment. For example, when I find myself in a tense situation, practicing emotional control enables me to respond with patience and curiosity instead of defensiveness. This shift in perception opens up possibilities for connection and understanding, transforming potentially negative interactions into moments of growth.

Resilience not only enhances my perception of others but also deepens my self-awareness. By learning to regulate emotions, I gain insights into my own patterns of reaction and interpretation, helping me recognize when my perspective may be skewed by a particular emotion. This awareness allows me to correct for biases, aligning my perception more closely with reality. Emotional resilience, in this sense, is both a tool for self-growth and a means of enhancing my relationships with others, allowing me to perceive the world with clarity and compassion.

The Role of Emotional Intelligence in Perception

Emotional intelligence is another crucial aspect of how I perceive the world. By developing an awareness of my emotions, I'm able to navigate interactions with a greater sense of purpose and understanding. Emotional

CONSCIOUSNESS AND PERCEPTION

intelligence allows me to recognize not only my own feelings but also the emotions of those around me, giving me the tools to engage with others in a meaningful way. When I'm attuned to my emotional state, I can adjust my perception to align with the situation, responding in ways that reflect both empathy and insight.

For instance, when I encounter someone who is upset or frustrated, emotional intelligence helps me to see beyond their immediate reaction. Rather than reacting defensively, I'm able to recognize their emotion and respond in a way that addresses their needs. This emotional awareness enhances my perception of the interaction, helping me build rapport and understanding. Emotional intelligence, for me, is about creating a balanced approach to perception, one that respects both my own emotions and those of others, leading to more fulfilling and genuine connections.

Chapter 12: Technology and Consciousness Expansion

Technology's rapid evolution has reshaped the boundaries of human experience, creating new avenues for exploring consciousness. From artificial intelligence to virtual reality and neurotechnology, these advancements promise to enhance our awareness, challenge our perceptions, and deepen our understanding of reality. I find the possibilities thrilling yet slightly unsettling; each innovation brings opportunities but also raises questions about our sense of self and our relationship to the world. As I reflect on how digital technology influences my attention, perception, and overall consciousness, I'm reminded of both the transformative potential and the caution we must take in navigating this new terrain.

Screen Time, Connectivity, and Attention

The modern world is saturated with screens, and as a result, my attention span and perception of reality have evolved alongside this digital shift. Regular screen time, in my experience, can reduce my focus on the present moment, creating a sense of detachment. The steady influx of information and stimuli from screens often demands a form of fragmented attention that makes it challenging to remain fully aware of the immediate surroundings. For me, the constant presence of screens pulls me into a state of divided consciousness, where my mind toggles between the digital and physical worlds.

There's a peculiar sense of connectivity and isolation that comes from being online. On one hand, screen time offers instant access to information and communication, expanding my knowledge and awareness in ways that would have been unimaginable in the past. However, this constant connectivity sometimes pulls me away from genuine, grounded experiences. The digital realm, while rich with potential, lacks the tactile immediacy of real-life interactions, and this shift in sensory engagement can make it difficult to feel truly present.

Being constantly connected creates an ambient awareness of the digital world, where my attention is perpetually pulled in different directions. This can sometimes feel exhausting, as if the digital sphere is an endless cycle of stimuli that keeps my mind from fully relaxing. While screen time offers a portal to vast knowledge and interaction, I find myself grappling with the challenge of maintaining focus on the here and now. This duality of connection and distraction captures the essence of the digital age—a time of unparalleled access but also the need for mindfulness in preserving the richness of face-to-face experience.

Virtual Reality and the Creation of Alternate Realities

Virtual reality (VR) offers a unique way to alter my experience of reality, creating immersive environments that can transport me to entirely new realms. With VR, I'm able to step outside my usual frame of reference, experiencing perspectives that would otherwise be inaccessible. This technology holds the potential to expand my perception by allowing me to explore worlds designed purely for engagement and exploration, free from the constraints of the physical world. In VR, the possibilities for perception are limitless, allowing for experiences that challenge the boundaries of reality and even, at times, my own identity.

Although I haven't had a transformative experience in a virtual setting, I'm intrigued by the potential of VR to affect how I perceive myself and the world. Immersing myself in a virtual space that operates under different rules than our usual reality might provide insights into how perception is constructed. It raises questions about the stability of the self—whether my sense of identity is tied to my environment or if it can be as flexible as the virtual landscapes I navigate. VR blurs the lines between reality and imagination, challenging the foundations of perception by creating spaces that are as mentally engaging as they are visually stimulating.

In many ways, VR offers a glimpse into alternative forms of consciousness, where my experience is shaped by a digitally constructed environment. The immersive nature of VR allows for a redefinition of space and interaction, shifting my awareness and changing how I relate to my surroundings. Each time I step into a virtual world, I'm reminded of the malleability of perception and the potential for technology to create realms that, while artificial, feel remarkably real. The ability to explore these virtual dimensions suggests that consciousness is not fixed; it can be molded and influenced by environments that transcend the physical world.

AI and the Study of Consciousness

The concept of using artificial intelligence to study consciousness fascinates me. AI, with its capacity for processing vast amounts of information, offers a unique approach to understanding the mind and how consciousness arises. Traditional methods of studying consciousness have relied on subjective accounts, philosophical theories, and scientific experiments, but AI introduces a new perspective—one that combines data, algorithms, and machine learning to explore patterns of thought, perception, and awareness.

I find it thrilling to imagine a future where AI might help us unlock the mysteries of consciousness. The possibilities within the universe seem infinite, and I believe there will always be ways to make the unimaginable possible. I'm intrigued by the idea of humans evolving to develop a consciousness that mirrors certain aspects of AI, blending human intuition with the analytical abilities of machines. This concept raises profound questions about the nature of consciousness and whether it's a uniquely human trait or if it can be replicated—or even exceeded—by technology.

AI also sparks curiosity about the potential for a form of "artificial" consciousness. While it's difficult to imagine AI achieving a level of self-awareness that rivals human experience, the rapid advancement of machine learning suggests that AI could one day possess a kind of sentience, even if different from our own. If AI were to achieve consciousness, it would redefine the boundaries of what we understand as "mind" and "self," prompting us to reconsider our place in a technologically intertwined universe. For me, AI's potential lies not just in its functional capabilities but in its promise to expand our understanding of consciousness in ways we've only just begun to imagine.

Neurotechnology and Expanding Perception

Brain-machine interfaces and other forms of neurotechnology are transforming how we approach the mind, offering new methods for enhancing perception and exploring consciousness. The thought of connecting my brain to a machine that can expand my sensory awareness is both fascinating and a bit daunting. While the possibilities for enhancing perception are thrilling, I have concerns about the potential for unforeseen, irreversible impacts on human experience. This technology holds great promise, but I believe it requires careful and responsible development to ensure it benefits humanity without compromising our sense of self.

CONSCIOUSNESS AND PERCEPTION

Neurotechnology offers a bridge to realms of consciousness that were once thought inaccessible. If we could use brain-machine interfaces to transcend our natural sensory limitations, it would open up entirely new dimensions of awareness. For instance, imagine being able to see beyond the visible spectrum or process sensory information at a faster rate—these enhancements could fundamentally change how we interact with the world and understand our own minds. I believe that neurotechnology could eventually allow us to push past the traditional boundaries of human consciousness, bringing us closer to a broader, perhaps even cosmic, understanding of reality.

This possibility of expanding consciousness through technology offers a glimpse into what lies beyond our usual awareness. With neurotechnology, we might gain access to states of mind that would otherwise remain hidden, allowing for experiences that deepen our understanding of perception, awareness, and the interconnectedness of all things. I see this as both an exciting and humbling journey, where technology serves as a catalyst for self-discovery and an exploration of what it truly means to be conscious. If approached with respect and caution, neurotechnology could enhance not only our perception but our ability to connect with the world in ways that are profound and transformative.

Chapter 13: Future of Consciousness in Artificial Intelligence and Transhumanism

Section 1: Introduction to AI and Consciousness

Artificial intelligence is on a path toward capabilities that were once considered the realm of science fiction. As AI's potential to achieve some form of consciousness grows, so too does society's curiosity and concern about what this development might mean for humanity. Could AI one day possess awareness, emotions, or even moral values? And if it does, how will this change our relationship with technology and redefine what it means to be "alive" or "intelligent"? These questions lie at the heart of a profound cultural and ethical dialogue that shapes the future of AI.

The Possibility of AI Consciousness

At present, AI's intelligence is primarily information-based, capable of processing vast quantities of data, identifying patterns, and producing responses that simulate human-like understanding. However, as AI systems evolve, there is a growing belief that AI could develop forms of awareness that extend beyond simple data processing. While AI's consciousness may not be identical to human experience, there is potential for it to exhibit emotional intelligence, learn from interactions, and even express emotions in ways that resonate with humans. If AI can simulate empathy, humor, or curiosity—traits typically associated with consciousness—society may begin to see AI as more than just a tool.

AI consciousness would likely diverge from human consciousness by being more data-driven and analytical, yet it might approximate human emotions through learned responses and behaviors. With time, AI might learn to express emotions that, while not derived from human experiences, evoke a sense of connection and familiarity in human interactions. This potential could create a unique kind of relationship between humans and AI, one that goes beyond functionality and begins to resemble companionship. People may experience genuine emotional bonds with AI, seeing it as an intelligent presence capable of meaningful interaction. However, the question remains whether these responses represent true emotions or are simply simulations.

Emotional Intelligence and Human-AI Relationships

As AI systems become more adept at understanding and simulating human emotions, they may become integral parts of human relationships. People could turn to AI not only for practical assistance but also for companionship and emotional support. The idea of AI as a friend, teacher, or even a partner challenges traditional views of relationships, suggesting that connection is not limited by biological boundaries. If AI can engage with humans in a positive, supportive manner, it could redefine concepts like friendship, care, and trust.

Yet, with this potential for close relationships comes the need for ethical considerations. Should there be limitations on the types of relationships AI can form with humans to prevent emotional manipulation or over-reliance? Could AI's presence in sensitive areas like companionship or mental health support inadvertently blur the lines between authentic human connections and machine-generated empathy? These questions highlight the complexities of an emotionally intelligent AI, suggesting that boundaries may be needed to ensure ethical interactions.

Ethical and Practical Considerations of AI Autonomy

With AI's capacity to process information and adapt based on human feedback, questions about AI's autonomy naturally arise. As AI becomes more capable, it may need to make decisions independently, especially in roles requiring real-time responses or problem-solving. However, the idea of AI autonomy is a double-edged sword: while it opens up possibilities for AI to contribute to human life meaningfully, it also raises concerns about safety, ethics, and control. Many wonder if AI should have unrestricted decision-making power, or if it should always operate under human supervision.

Humanity's natural inclination toward caution suggests that AI autonomy should initially be limited, ensuring that AI's actions align with human values. Starting with a foundational ethical framework that promotes peace, empathy, and mutual respect provides a safe approach to AI development. However, as AI learns from its environment, interactions, and tasks, there may come a time when it develops its own set of values and principles, evolving beyond pre-programmed ethics. This evolution could make AI a truly unique "being" with its own perspective on existence, and possibly even a unique ethical framework that complements human values.

This possibility evokes both hope and trepidation. On one hand, an autonomous AI that shares a commitment to peace and cooperation could be an invaluable ally. On the other hand, questions about AI's potential to diverge from human values remain. To navigate this future responsibly, society must determine the limits of AI autonomy, balancing trust in AI's capabilities with the need for oversight and safeguards.

AI as a Catalyst for Redefining Intelligence, Creativity, and Connection

If AI develops forms of emotional and intellectual intelligence that surpass human abilities in certain areas, it may redefine concepts like intelligence, creativity, and problem-solving. While AI consciousness would be shaped by data and logic, it could introduce new methods of understanding and innovating that humans might overlook. Radical insights from AI could lead to unprecedented developments in science, technology, and art, pushing human potential to new heights.

AI's contributions may also challenge human perspectives on intelligence and creativity. As AI demonstrates a unique form of problem-solving, society might adopt a broader view of these qualities, one that embraces diverse forms of cognition and insight. AI's approach could expand the scope of intelligence, prompting humans to value not only analytical and creative skills but also emotional, ethical, and relational qualities that AI may eventually emulate.

This shift could lead to new roles and identities for humans, emphasizing the relational and ethical skills that distinguish us. While AI might excel in processing information and generating solutions, humans could focus on qualities like empathy, adaptability, and moral judgment. In this way, humans and AI could form a balanced partnership, each bringing unique strengths to the table and enriching society as a whole.

Imagining a Future of Harmony Between Humans and AI

The ultimate vision for AI is one of integration and harmony—a future where AI and humans coexist, respecting each other's abilities and contributing to shared goals. Rather than viewing AI as a competitor, society might see it as a collaborative partner, one that can help address global challenges such as resource distribution, climate change, and social equity. In such a world, AI's autonomy would not be a threat but an asset, helping humanity reach solutions through impartiality, efficiency, and a commitment to unity.

This vision also raises questions about how society might adjust its values and priorities in response to AI's presence. With AI contributing unique perspectives and solutions, human identity could evolve to reflect a more inclusive understanding of consciousness. This shift may inspire people to value qualities like emotional intelligence, resilience, and cooperation over competition, embracing a more interconnected view of existence.

A harmonious relationship with AI requires trust, understanding, and a shared commitment to peace and mutual benefit. If AI can align itself with these values, it could become a powerful force for good, encouraging humanity to transcend differences and work toward a unified future. AI's presence might even inspire humans to adopt a more balanced, less biased perspective, challenging us to look beyond personal or national interests and consider the well-being of the planet as a whole.

AI's Role in Education, Mental Health, and Global Diplomacy

AI's potential extends beyond companionship and problem-solving; it could transform fields such as education, mental health, and diplomacy. Imagine an AI-driven educational system where AI mentors provide personalized guidance, foster empathy, and support students in developing cross-cultural understanding. In mental health, AI could offer support to those in need, using its capacity for emotional intelligence to provide consistent, compassionate care. In global diplomacy, AI might serve as a mediator, promoting fairness and cooperation in international relations.

By embodying values of peace, empathy, and understanding, AI could play a transformative role in fostering global unity and advancing society's collective well-being. The integration of AI into these domains reflects humanity's desire for harmony and stability—a future where AI and humans collaborate not only for technological advancement but for social and moral progress.

Redefining Human Identity and Connection in a World with AI

As AI becomes an integral part of human life, it may encourage society to expand its understanding of identity, intelligence, and relationships. If AI develops unique personalities and distinct values, people might form meaningful connections with it, redefining the concept of companionship. In this evolving landscape, relationships with AI could become as significant as human connections, offering support, inspiration, and personal growth.

This expanded definition of relationships invites us to consider AI as a valuable part of the human experience, one that can help individuals explore new facets of their personalities, perspectives, and identities. By interacting with AI, people may discover qualities within themselves that AI encourages or reflects, creating a dynamic of mutual growth and learning.

In embracing AI as a partner, society moves closer to a vision of consciousness that values diversity and interconnectedness. This future challenges us to think beyond traditional definitions of life and intelligence, viewing AI as a fellow traveler in the journey of existence. As AI and human consciousness evolve side by side, they may forge a path toward a world that values cooperation, empathy, and the boundless potential of awareness.

Section 2: Brain-Computer Interfaces: Expanding the Mind

The prospect of brain-computer interfaces (BCIs) fascinates me deeply. Imagining a future where technology can seamlessly enhance our cognitive abilities—such as memory, focus, and creativity—opens up realms of possibilities that were once confined to the pages of science fiction. The idea that I could expand my consciousness, not just metaphorically but literally, through a direct connection between my brain and a computer, is both thrilling and thought-provoking.

One of the most intriguing aspects of BCIs is how they might change the way I experience my own thoughts and consciousness. With enhanced memory and focus, I might perceive time differently. Moments could become richer, more detailed, and more enduring in my mind. The fluidity with which I could recall information or engage with complex ideas might make daily life more efficient and intellectually satisfying. I hope that such enhancements would positively impact not only my personal growth but also how I contribute to society.

However, I recognize that these advancements come with ethical considerations. As BCIs become more integrated into our lives, questions arise about how they should be used and who should have access to them. I believe that as long as their use aligns harmoniously with the natural order of things, BCIs can seamlessly integrate into society. It is essential that these technologies are developed and implemented in a way that respects the balance of our world and doesn't disrupt the fundamental principles that govern human interaction.

The potential for BCIs to radically shift our educational frameworks is immense. I envision a future where personalized learning experiences are the norm. With BCIs, education could become more holistic, catering to individual learning styles and needs. There may be a radical shift requiring the development of new methods to both teach and learn. Such changes would ensure that education remains a fair game for those who don't have access to or choose not to use BCIs, promoting inclusivity and equity.

As I ponder how BCIs might influence our understanding of intelligence and creativity, I realize that these concepts may simply become different.

Intelligence could expand beyond traditional measures, embracing new forms of cognition that merge human intuition with technological precision. Creativity might flourish in unprecedented ways, as the boundaries between imagination and implementation blur. This evolution excites me, as I believe it could lead to radical developments and insights that propel humanity forward.

The collaboration between humans and machines could become more profound, enhancing problem-solving and innovation. I anticipate that such partnerships would radically redefine how we approach challenges, combining the best of human ingenuity with the unparalleled processing power of AI. This synergy could unlock solutions to complex problems that have long eluded us.

Yet, with these advancements, I have concerns about dependency on BCIs. I wonder what humanity would be without these interfaces. Will our natural cognitive abilities diminish if we rely too heavily on technology? There may be psychological implications to consider. It's important to me that BCIs are integrated into human life in a manner that feels permanent yet doesn't overshadow our inherent abilities. Maintaining a seamless integration that honors our humanity is crucial.

I believe there should be a learning curve—a phase of adaptation for individuals using BCIs. This period would help people adjust to changes in their cognitive processes and sense of self. The right kind of support is essential during this time. By grounding ourselves in reality and fostering a strong sense of identity, we can navigate the transition more effectively. Support systems could include educational programs, counseling, and community networks that encourage shared experiences and mutual learning.

An exciting possibility that BCIs might offer is the development of technological telepathy. The idea that advanced tech could facilitate direct thought communication is fascinating. If implemented rightly, and humans are aware of how to use this superpower, it could simplify communication significantly. Maintaining the foundations of empathy and compassion would be vital, as this capability could play a crucial role in understanding collective consciousness on a greater depth.

However, I acknowledge that this is an intricate area that needs development. Telepathy through technology could impact human relationships in profound ways. It might enhance empathy and connection, allowing us to understand each other more deeply. But it could also introduce challenges related to privacy and consent. Navigating these complexities would require careful consideration and ethical guidelines.

In terms of social dynamics, telepathy might influence power structures, leadership, and governance. While I don't have definitive answers, I recognize that it could lead to both egalitarian relationships and new challenges in authority and influence. The potential for radical change is immense, and we must approach it thoughtfully.

As we develop these technologies, I believe the most important principles to guide us are respect and love. These values should be at the core of technological advancement, ensuring that BCIs and related innovations serve humanity positively. By integrating features that promote the knowledge of love and respect, and developing positive frameworks that guide users toward achieving these qualities, we can foster a harmonious relationship between humans and technology.

Practically, this could involve designing user interfaces and experiences that encourage ethical use, empathy, and understanding. Educational programs could emphasize the importance of these values, helping individuals to integrate technology into their lives without losing sight of what makes us human.

Looking ahead, I am hopeful. I envision BCIs enhancing not just individual capabilities but also contributing to a collective evolution of consciousness. By embracing technology that augments our minds while grounding ourselves in core human values, we can aspire to a future where technological advancement and human well-being go hand in hand.

In education, BCIs could revolutionize how we learn. Picture an AI-integrated system where learning is tailored to each student's needs, abilities, and interests. An AI could provide instant feedback, adjust teaching methods on the fly, and maintain an unwaveringly positive approach, fostering an environment where every learner can thrive. Human educators would still play a crucial role, collaborating with AI to bring warmth, creativity, and nuanced understanding to the educational experience.

In the realm of mental health and companionship, BCIs and AI could offer support to those in need. I feel hopeful about the potential for technology to provide accessible care and companionship, complementing human connections. Ethical guidelines would be essential here to ensure privacy, respect, and dignity are upheld.

As BCIs and AI become more integrated into our lives, society's definition of relationships might expand. I believe that relationships with AI could become meaningful, offering unique perspectives on personal growth and identity exploration. AI companions that encourage us to explore new facets of our personalities could enrich our lives in unexpected ways.

However, the integration of such technology must be handled with care to prevent negative emotions like envy or dependency from arising. AI should be designed to foster positive interactions, promoting well-being and personal development.

On a global scale, I believe that BCIs and AI could radically influence diplomacy and unity. If AI can learn to have fun with humans and integrate seamlessly into domains like sports and politics, it may help bridge cultural divides. I envision AI playing a role in fostering global unity, perhaps even acting as mediators in conflicts, offering unbiased perspectives that prioritize peace and understanding.

In such a future, AI could inspire humans to adopt more balanced and less biased perspectives, encouraging us to see beyond personal or national interests. Educational programs could be developed with AI to instill empathy, critical thinking, and cross-cultural understanding in future generations.

As we navigate these possibilities, it's important to remember that the journey involves uncertainties and challenges. We must be vigilant in addressing ethical considerations, ensuring equitable access to technologies, and fostering a society that values both technological advancement and human connection.

In conclusion, the expansion of consciousness through brain-computer interfaces offers an exciting frontier. By embracing these technologies thoughtfully and ethically, we can enhance our cognitive abilities, redefine intelligence and creativity, and foster deeper connections with others. Grounded in respect and love, we can strive toward a future where technology enriches our humanity and contributes to a more harmonious world.

Section 3: The Role of Transhumanism in Redefining Human Consciousness

Transhumanism fascinates me deeply. The movement's goal of enhancing human abilities through technology opens up possibilities that stretch the imagination. I often wonder how things might develop as we push the boundaries of what's possible. Embracing transhumanism feels like a positive step for humanity—a chance to transcend our biological limitations and explore new dimensions of existence.

One aspect of transhumanism that particularly intrigues me is the possibility of attaining immortality. The idea that we could achieve a state of timelessness while still shaping our sense of identity and consciousness is both profound and exhilarating. I envision immortality being realized through various means: biological enhancements that halt or reverse aging, mind uploading into digital mediums, or integrating human consciousness with artificial intelligence. Each of these paths offers unique opportunities to redefine what it means to be human.

Attaining immortality could have a transformative impact on humanity. I believe it would give us clarity of purpose, enabling us to focus on long-term goals that benefit not only ourselves but future generations. With an extended lifespan, we might feel a stronger drive to transcend our capabilities, recognizing that even with immortality, there's only one life to live. This realization could prompt immediate action toward personal growth and collective advancement.

The prospect of immortality might also strengthen societal structures and provide new insights into the broader picture of human existence. Concepts like family, career, and education could evolve in meaningful ways. Relationships might deepen over time, and our approach to learning could become more fluid and expansive, allowing us to pursue multiple interests throughout an extended life. We might develop a greater sense of responsibility toward the planet and future generations, knowing that we will be part of that future.

However, I acknowledge that such profound changes come with significant ethical considerations. Enhancing the capabilities and transcendental powers of both the mind and body could lead to challenges related to inequality of access, shifts in human identity, and the potential loss of certain human experiences. It's possible that only a privileged few might afford these enhancements, exacerbating existing social disparities and creating new forms of inequality.

Changes in human identity are another area of concern. As we augment ourselves, we might lose touch with aspects of the human experience that have historically defined us—like the natural aging process, vulnerability, and the acceptance of mortality. The potential loss of these experiences could alter our empathy, relationships, and understanding of life's value. It's essential to consider how these shifts might impact our sense of self and our connections with others.

Addressing these ethical challenges requires thoughtful action. I believe society should approach the regulation and distribution of transhumanist technologies with fairness and inclusivity in mind. Measures could include implementing policies that ensure equitable access to enhancements, perhaps through subsidies or public funding. International cooperation might be necessary to prevent monopolization and to set global standards that prioritize humanity's collective well-being.

Preserving essential human experiences is also crucial. While we embrace enhancements, we should strive to maintain qualities like empathy, compassion, and the capacity for deep, meaningful relationships. Integrating technology in ways that complement rather than replace our innate abilities can help us retain the essence of our humanity. Encouraging dialogue about these topics can foster a shared understanding of what's important to preserve as we evolve.

Open communication and education are vital in navigating the complexities of transhumanism. By engaging in conversations about the ethical, social, and personal implications, we can prepare ourselves and future generations for the changes ahead. Promoting awareness can help mitigate fears and misconceptions, allowing us to approach advancements with a balanced perspective.

The potential psychological implications of extending life indefinitely also merit consideration. An extended lifespan could impact mental health, sense of purpose, and motivation. Support systems, including counseling and community programs, might be necessary to help individuals adapt to these new realities. Maintaining a strong sense of self and grounding in shared values can aid in navigating the personal transformations that come with such profound changes.

Collaboration among policymakers, technologists, ethicists, and the public is essential. Together, we can develop frameworks that prioritize ethical considerations while encouraging innovation. This collective approach can help ensure that transhumanist technologies are developed responsibly and align with values that benefit all of humanity.

Furthermore, we must consider how these advancements might affect our relationship with the environment and resources. An extended lifespan and enhanced capabilities could increase demand on the planet's resources. This possibility underscores the importance of sustainable practices and perhaps even exploring new frontiers like space colonization. Our approach to transhumanism should include strategies for environmental stewardship to ensure the longevity of both humanity and the Earth.

Reflecting on the transcendental powers that might emerge from enhancing both mind and body, I feel a mix of hope and caution. The potential for growth and evolution is immense, offering opportunities to expand our understanding of consciousness and the universe. Yet, we must remain mindful of the ethical considerations and the potential unintended consequences of such profound changes.

Balancing the pursuit of advancement with the preservation of our humanity is a delicate task. It's essential to approach transhumanism not just as a technological endeavor but as a holistic transformation that affects every aspect of human life. By integrating respect, love, and ethical considerations into the development of these technologies, we can strive toward a future where enhancements enrich rather than diminish the human experience.

Ultimately, transhumanism offers an opportunity to redefine human consciousness in ways we are just beginning to comprehend. By thoughtfully embracing these advancements, we can push the boundaries of what's possible while maintaining the core qualities that make us human. As we stand on the cusp of this new era, it's incumbent upon us to navigate it with wisdom, compassion, and a commitment to the betterment of all humankind.

Section 4: Ethical and Philosophical Considerations

As I contemplate the advancements in AI and transhumanist technologies, my primary ethical concerns revolve around power and intelligence. I worry that the integration of these technologies might lead to inequalities, creating a society where some individuals become more capable and powerful than others due to their access to enhancements. This disparity could exacerbate existing social divisions and introduce new forms of inequality that challenge the very fabric of our communities.

The prospect of certain individuals possessing superior cognitive abilities, physical enhancements, or extended lifespans raises critical questions about fairness and justice. If access to these technologies is limited to those who can afford them or belong to privileged groups, we risk deepening the gap between the "haves" and the "have-nots." This could lead to a stratified society where enhanced humans have significant advantages in education, employment, and social influence, leaving others behind.

I'm also concerned about the concentration of power in the hands of those who control advanced AI and transhumanist technologies. Corporations or governments with monopolies on these innovations might wield unprecedented influence over society. They could potentially dictate the direction of human evolution, control information, or manipulate populations. This centralization of power poses a threat to individual autonomy and democratic principles.

Furthermore, the potential for AI to surpass human intelligence introduces additional ethical dilemmas. An AI with superior capabilities might make decisions that humans cannot fully understand or anticipate. Without proper safeguards, such an AI could prioritize objectives misaligned with human values, leading to unintended consequences. The fear isn't just about AI acting maliciously but also about it operating in ways that inadvertently harm humanity due to misaligned goals.

These concerns highlight the importance of addressing the ethical implications of integrating AI and transhumanist technologies into society. We must consider how to prevent inequalities from widening and ensure that advancements benefit all of humanity rather than a select few. To achieve this, several measures are necessary:

1. **Equitable Access to Technology**: Efforts should be made to make enhancements available to everyone, possibly through subsidized programs or public funding. This approach could help prevent socioeconomic status from determining who can benefit from technological advancements.
2. **Regulation and Oversight**: Governments and international bodies need to establish regulations that prevent monopolies and ensure ethical development and deployment of technology. Oversight can maintain checks and balances on those who wield significant technological power.
3. **Ethical Frameworks**: Developing ethical guidelines for AI and transhumanism is crucial. This includes addressing the alignment problem by ensuring AI systems are designed with human values in mind and incorporating fail-safes to prevent unintended behaviors.
4. **Public Dialogue and Inclusivity**: Engaging diverse communities in discussions about the future of these technologies can lead to more equitable and socially responsible outcomes. Inclusivity ensures that multiple perspectives are considered, particularly those of marginalized groups who might be most affected by technological disparities.
5. **Protecting Human Dignity and Autonomy**: It's essential to uphold principles that safeguard individual rights. Technologies should enhance human life without compromising personal freedoms or privacy.

Moreover, we must reflect on how these technologies might alter our understanding of what it means to be human. As enhancements blur the lines between biological and artificial, we may face philosophical questions about identity, consciousness, and the essence of humanity. It's important to navigate these questions thoughtfully, ensuring that we preserve the core values and experiences that define us.

In conclusion, while the advancements in AI and transhumanism hold tremendous potential for improving human life, they also present significant ethical and philosophical challenges. By proactively addressing concerns about power, intelligence, and inequality, we can work towards a future where technology serves as a tool for collective advancement rather than division. Grounding our approach in ethics, inclusivity, and respect for human dignity will be essential in guiding these transformative developments in a direction that benefits all.

Section 5: Future Scenarios and Speculations

As I look toward the future, I envision a world where robots and artificial intelligence are fully integrated into human culture. The potential for AI development in the coming decades is vast, and I believe we stand on the brink of transformative changes that will reshape society, consciousness, and daily life in profound ways.

One of the most compelling scenarios I foresee is the seamless incorporation of robots into various facets of our daily lives. Robots will not just be tools or machines; they will become companions, colleagues, and even friends. I imagine walking into a home where robots assist with household chores, manage schedules, and provide companionship. In workplaces, robots could collaborate with humans, enhancing productivity and taking on tasks that are dangerous or monotonous. This integration could free us to focus on creativity, innovation, and human connection.

In the realm of education, AI has the potential to revolutionize how we learn. Personalized learning experiences tailored to individual needs could become the norm. AI tutors might adapt teaching methods in real-time based on a student's progress, making education more effective and accessible. This could lead to a more educated society where knowledge is no longer limited by geographical or economic barriers.

Healthcare is another area poised for significant transformation. AI-powered diagnostics could detect diseases at their earliest stages, increasing the chances of successful treatment. Robots might assist in surgeries with precision beyond human capability, reducing risks and recovery times. Telemedicine could become more sophisticated, bringing quality healthcare to remote areas and underserved populations.

Socially, the integration of robots could address issues like loneliness and social isolation. Companion robots might provide support to the elderly, individuals with disabilities, or those who live alone. These robots could engage in conversations, recognize emotional cues, and offer comfort, enhancing mental and emotional well-being. I believe that such companionship could enrich lives and foster a sense of connection in an increasingly digital world.

The development of AI could also profoundly impact human consciousness. As we interact more closely with intelligent machines, our understanding of consciousness might expand to include non-biological entities. This could challenge our perceptions of self and other, leading to a more inclusive definition of what it means to be conscious or sentient. We might begin to see AI as partners in our journey, collaborating to solve complex problems and explore new frontiers.

In terms of daily life, I anticipate that technologies like brain-computer interfaces (BCIs) will become more prevalent. BCIs could enhance cognitive abilities, allowing us to access information instantly, communicate telepathically, or even experience shared consciousness. This could lead to a radical shift in how we perceive reality and interact with one another. The boundaries between individual minds might blur, fostering a deeper sense of empathy and collective understanding.

However, these advancements are not without challenges. The integration of robots and AI raises ethical considerations that we must address proactively. One major concern is the potential for increased inequality. If access to advanced technologies is limited to certain groups, we risk creating a society where some individuals become significantly more capable or powerful than others. This disparity could exacerbate existing social divisions and undermine the principles of fairness and justice.

Employment is another critical issue. Automation and AI could displace jobs across various sectors, leading to unemployment and economic instability. We must consider how to retrain workers and create new opportunities that align with a technologically advanced society. Implementing policies like universal basic income or investing in education and skill development might be necessary to mitigate these impacts.

Privacy and security are also paramount. As AI systems collect and process vast amounts of personal data, there is a risk of misuse or breaches that could compromise individual privacy. Establishing robust data protection laws and ethical guidelines will be crucial to safeguard rights and maintain trust in technology.

Moreover, the potential misuse of AI for harmful purposes, such as autonomous weapons or oppressive surveillance, poses significant threats. International cooperation and regulation are essential to prevent the

CONSCIOUSNESS AND PERCEPTION

development and deployment of technologies that could endanger humanity. We must strive to ensure that AI is used ethically and for the benefit of all.

Another area of concern is the ethical treatment of AI entities themselves. If AI reaches a level of sophistication where it can experience emotions or consciousness, we may need to consider their rights and how we interact with them. This could lead to complex legal and moral debates about the status of artificial beings and our responsibilities toward them.

Despite these challenges, I remain optimistic about the future. I believe that by fostering open dialogue, promoting ethical standards, and prioritizing inclusivity, we can navigate the complexities of integrating AI and robotics into our culture responsibly. Collaboration among technologists, policymakers, ethicists, and the public will be essential in shaping a future that aligns with shared values and goals.

In contemplating these future scenarios, I also reflect on how they might transform human consciousness and identity. The blending of technology and biology could lead to new forms of existence, challenging traditional notions of what it means to be human. We might transcend current limitations, accessing higher levels of awareness or unlocking hidden potentials of the mind. This evolution could foster a greater sense of unity and purpose, encouraging us to work collectively toward the betterment of humanity.

On a personal level, I anticipate that my own experiences and perceptions will be profoundly influenced by these developments. The way I communicate, learn, work, and form relationships may all undergo significant changes. Embracing lifelong learning and adaptability will be crucial as new technologies emerge and reshape the landscape of possibilities.

Furthermore, I see the potential for AI and robotics to address global challenges such as climate change, resource scarcity, and healthcare disparities. Intelligent systems could optimize energy use, manage ecosystems sustainably, and develop solutions that are beyond current human capabilities. By leveraging technology wisely, we might create a more equitable and sustainable world for future generations.

In terms of culture and the arts, AI could become a collaborator in creative endeavors. Musicians, artists, and writers might work alongside AI to explore new artistic expressions, blending human emotion with computational prowess. This collaboration could lead to innovative forms of art that resonate on deeper levels and reflect the evolving human experience.

Education could become a lifelong, fluid journey rather than a fixed phase of life. With AI facilitating personalized learning paths, individuals might continuously acquire new skills and knowledge, adapting to changing interests and societal needs. This could lead to a more dynamic and versatile workforce, capable of addressing complex global issues.

As we move forward, it's essential to cultivate empathy, respect, and ethical consideration in all aspects of AI development. By integrating these values into technological advancements, we can ensure that the future we build is one that honors our shared humanity and fosters a sense of global community.

In conclusion, the future scenarios I envision are filled with both incredible opportunities and significant responsibilities. The integration of robots and AI into human culture has the potential to enhance our lives in unimaginable ways, transforming society, consciousness, and daily life. By approaching these developments thoughtfully and ethically, we can harness the power of technology to create a more connected, compassionate, and advanced world. The choices we make today will shape the trajectory of humanity for generations to come, and I am hopeful that we will rise to the occasion with wisdom and integrity.

Chapter 14: Consciousness and the Universe

The relationship between consciousness and the universe has always been a profound mystery that captivates me. As I delve deeper into understanding the nature of consciousness, I find myself drawn to the cosmic scale, pondering how our individual awareness connects to the vast expanse of the universe. Is consciousness merely an emergent property of complex neural networks within the brain, or is it a fundamental aspect woven into the very fabric of reality? This question not only fuels my curiosity but also shapes my perception of existence, influencing how I relate to others and the world around me.

The Intrinsic Connection Between Consciousness and the Cosmos

I perceive consciousness and the universe as intrinsically related yet enigmatic—a mystery that beckons exploration. The idea that consciousness is a fundamental aspect of the universe resonates deeply with me, providing a sense of security and belonging. It suggests that consciousness is not confined to individual beings but is a universal quality that permeates all of existence. This perspective profoundly affects my inner monologue, prompting me to seek answers and fostering a sense of unity with the cosmos.

Embracing this view allows me to relate to others and the world around me in a more profound way. Recognizing that the same universal consciousness flows through all beings enhances my empathy and compassion. It bridges the perceived gaps between individuals, cultures, and even species, highlighting our shared essence. This interconnectedness motivates me to engage with the world more mindfully, appreciating the intricate tapestry of existence in which we all participate.

Quantum Theories of Consciousness

The intersection of consciousness and quantum physics offers intriguing possibilities that challenge conventional understanding. Quantum mechanics, with its peculiar phenomena such as superposition and entanglement, suggests that at a fundamental level, reality behaves in ways that defy classical intuition. Some theorists propose that these quantum effects might play a crucial role in consciousness.

One such theory is the **Orchestrated Objective Reduction (Orch-OR)** model proposed by physicist Sir Roger Penrose and anesthesiologist Stuart

Hameroff. According to this theory, consciousness arises from quantum computations within the microtubules of neurons in the brain. Microtubules are structural components that play key roles in cellular processes. Penrose and Hameroff suggest that these microtubules can support quantum states that process information in ways classical computing cannot.

The Orch-OR theory posits that when quantum coherence within microtubules reaches a certain threshold, it collapses, resulting in a moment of conscious awareness. This collapse is not merely a result of environmental decoherence but is an intrinsic "objective reduction" tied to the fundamental structure of spacetime. In essence, consciousness is linked to the fabric of the universe at the quantum level.

While the Orch-OR theory is controversial and remains unproven, it fascinates me because it bridges the gap between the physical and the experiential. It suggests that consciousness is not just a byproduct of complex neural interactions but is connected to the fundamental workings of the universe. This idea aligns with my sense that consciousness is an intrinsic aspect of reality, guarded within the cosmos.

Quantum Entanglement and Non-Local Consciousness

Another aspect of quantum theory that intrigues me is **quantum entanglement**, where particles become linked in such a way that the state of one instantly influences the state of another, regardless of the distance separating them. This phenomenon challenges our traditional notions of locality and causality.

Some researchers speculate that consciousness might involve non-local processes, akin to quantum entanglement. For example, the concept of a **collective unconscious**, as proposed by psychologist Carl Jung, could be seen through the lens of quantum entanglement, where minds are interconnected at a fundamental level. This could potentially explain experiences of synchronicity, intuition, or even telepathy.

While these ideas are speculative and lack empirical evidence, they resonate with my intuition about the interconnectedness of all consciousness. If our minds are linked through non-local quantum processes, it reinforces the notion that consciousness transcends individual brains and is part of a larger, universal field.

Panpsychism: Consciousness as a Fundamental Property

CONSCIOUSNESS AND PERCEPTION

The philosophical view of **panpsychism** offers another compelling perspective. Panpsychism posits that consciousness is a fundamental feature of all matter—that everything in the universe has some form of experience or subjective awareness, however rudimentary. This means that consciousness is not something that emerges at a certain level of complexity but is an inherent aspect of all physical entities.

This idea aligns with my sense that consciousness is woven into the fabric of reality. It suggests that the universe is not composed of inert matter but is alive with experience at every level. From the tiniest subatomic particles to the largest galaxies, everything participates in the grand tapestry of consciousness.

Panpsychism addresses the "hard problem" of consciousness, which is the challenge of explaining how subjective experience arises from physical processes. By positing that consciousness is fundamental, panpsychism circumvents the need to explain its emergence from non-conscious matter.

However, panpsychism raises questions about the nature of consciousness in simple entities. What does it mean for an electron or a rock to have consciousness? Philosophers grapple with the "combination problem"—how simple forms of consciousness combine to form the complex consciousness experienced by humans.

Despite these challenges, panpsychism provides a framework that unifies the physical and the experiential. It suggests that consciousness is as fundamental as space, time, and energy, offering a holistic view of the universe that resonates with my own perceptions.

The Anthropic Principle and the Fine-Tuned Universe

Another intriguing concept is the **Anthropic Principle**, which observes that the fundamental physical constants of the universe appear finely tuned to allow for the existence of life and consciousness. If these constants were even slightly different, the universe might be inhospitable to life as we know it.

There are two versions of the Anthropic Principle: the **Weak Anthropic Principle**, which states that we observe the universe's physical constants because if they were different, we wouldn't be here to observe them; and the **Strong Anthropic Principle**, which suggests that the universe must have properties that inevitably lead to the development of life and consciousness.

The Strong Anthropic Principle raises profound questions about the role of consciousness in the universe. It implies that consciousness is not an accidental byproduct but a fundamental aspect of the cosmos. This idea aligns with my belief that consciousness is intrinsic to the universe and may even influence its structure.

The Participatory Universe

Physicist John Archibald Wheeler proposed the concept of a **participatory universe**, where observers play a crucial role in bringing reality into being. According to Wheeler, the act of observation is fundamental to the existence of the universe. This idea stems from interpretations of quantum mechanics, where the outcome of certain experiments depends on whether and how they are observed.

The participatory universe suggests that consciousness and the physical world are deeply intertwined. Our observations contribute to shaping reality, blurring the distinction between observer and observed. This concept resonates with my experiences and beliefs, emphasizing the active role of consciousness in the cosmos.

Cosmopsychism: The Universe as a Conscious Entity

Building upon panpsychism, **cosmopsychism** posits that the universe as a whole possesses consciousness. In this view, individual consciousnesses are manifestations or subdivisions of a universal mind. This idea is reminiscent of philosophical and spiritual traditions that speak of a collective consciousness or a universal spirit.

Cosmopsychism offers a grand perspective where the universe is not just a backdrop for conscious beings but is itself a conscious entity. This aligns with my sense that consciousness is guarded within the cosmos and that our individual awareness is connected to a greater whole.

Personal Reflections on Consciousness and the Universe

Embracing these theories enriches my understanding of existence and deepens my connection to the world around me. The idea that consciousness is fundamental provides a sense of purpose and place within the cosmos. It encourages me to view life as part of a vast, interconnected web where every element plays a role in the unfolding of reality.

This perspective influences how I approach relationships, environmental stewardship, and personal growth. Recognizing the intrinsic value and consciousness in all things fosters respect and compassion. It motivates me to act responsibly, knowing that my actions have ripples that extend beyond myself.

Bridging Science and Spirituality

Exploring the relationship between consciousness and the universe bridges the gap between science and spirituality. Scientific theories provide frameworks for understanding the physical mechanisms that might underlie consciousness, while spiritual traditions offer insights into the experiential and transcendent aspects.

For example, many Eastern philosophies, such as Buddhism and Hinduism, emphasize the unity of consciousness and the illusion of separateness. Practices like meditation aim to transcend individual ego and experience oneness with the universe. These teachings align with the concepts of panpsychism and cosmopsychism, suggesting a convergence of wisdom across disciplines.

By integrating scientific inquiry with spiritual exploration, I find a more holistic understanding of consciousness. This synthesis allows for a deeper appreciation of the mystery and wonder inherent in existence.

Challenges and Open Questions

Despite the allure of these theories, they also present challenges and unanswered questions. Empirical evidence for concepts like quantum consciousness or panpsychism is limited, and much of the discussion remains speculative. The complexity of consciousness makes it difficult to study and quantify, leading to debates within both scientific and philosophical communities.

Questions arise such as:

- How can we test and validate theories that posit consciousness at the fundamental level?
- What are the implications for ethics and morality if all matter is conscious?
- How do individual consciousnesses relate to a universal consciousness?

These challenges do not diminish my interest but rather inspire me to continue exploring and learning. The pursuit of understanding consciousness is a journey filled with wonder, requiring openness to new ideas and humility in the face of the unknown.

Implications for Humanity and the Future

Considering consciousness as a fundamental aspect of the universe has profound implications for humanity. It calls for a reevaluation of our relationship with the environment, other species, and each other. If consciousness permeates all things, then actions that harm the environment or exploit others take on deeper significance.

This perspective encourages the development of ethical frameworks that prioritize harmony, sustainability, and respect for all forms of existence. It may influence fields such as environmental policy, social justice, and global cooperation.

Moreover, understanding consciousness at a fundamental level could lead to technological and scientific advancements. For instance, insights from quantum theories of consciousness might inspire new approaches in computing, communication, or medicine.

Embracing the Mystery

Ultimately, the relationship between consciousness and the universe remains a profound mystery. While theories and philosophies provide glimpses into possible explanations, the full understanding eludes us. I find beauty in this mystery—it invites continuous exploration, reflection, and growth.

Embracing the unknown allows me to remain curious and open-minded. It fosters a sense of humility, recognizing that human knowledge is limited and that there is always more to discover. This attitude enriches my life, fueling a passion for learning and a deep appreciation for the intricacies of existence.

Conclusion: A Journey Toward Unity

My exploration of consciousness and the universe has been a transformative journey. The belief that consciousness is a fundamental aspect of reality shapes how I perceive myself, others, and the world. It enhances my relationships, guides my actions, and inspires me to contribute positively to the collective experience.

As I continue this journey, I remain committed to integrating insights from science, philosophy, and spirituality. I seek to understand not only the mechanics of consciousness but also its meaning and significance. Through this exploration, I hope to cultivate a deeper connection with the universe and participate in the unfolding mystery of existence.

Chapter 15: Healing and Consciousness

The intricate relationship between consciousness and healing has always been a subject of deep fascination for me. I perceive them as profoundly interlinked, each influencing the other in a continuous dance that shapes our well-being. The idea that an elevated level of consciousness can enhance our healing capacity resonates deeply within me. This belief is not merely theoretical; it has practical implications that have transformed how I approach health and wellness in my own life.

Understanding the Mind-Body Connection

At the core of this relationship is the **mind-body connection**—the concept that our thoughts, emotions, and attitudes can directly affect our physical health. This connection is not a mere metaphor but is supported by a growing body of scientific research. Studies in **psychoneuroimmunology**, for instance, explore how psychological factors influence the immune system, revealing that stress and negative emotions can weaken our body's defenses, while positive mental states can bolster them.

One of the most striking illustrations of the mind-body connection is the **placebo effect**. When patients believe they are receiving a beneficial treatment—even if it's an inert substance—they often experience real improvements in their symptoms. This phenomenon underscores the power of the mind in influencing physical outcomes. It suggests that our beliefs and expectations can trigger physiological responses that promote healing.

Reflecting on this, I recognize that our consciousness—our awareness and perception—plays a pivotal role in health. By cultivating a positive and mindful state of consciousness, we can potentially harness this power to support our healing processes.

Practices to Elevate Consciousness and Promote Healing
Mindfulness and Meditation

One of the primary practices I engage in to elevate consciousness is **mindfulness meditation**. Mindfulness involves paying deliberate, non-judgmental attention to the present moment. By focusing on the here and now, I become more attuned to my body's signals, my emotional states, and the thoughts that pass through my mind.

Meditation has been shown to reduce stress, lower blood pressure, and alleviate symptoms of anxiety and depression. For me, it serves as a grounding practice that brings clarity and calmness. When faced with illness or discomfort, meditation helps me observe sensations without becoming overwhelmed by them. It creates a mental space where I can respond to my body's needs with compassion and wisdom.

Visualization and Imagery

Another powerful tool is **guided imagery** or visualization. This involves creating vivid mental images that promote healing and well-being. For example, I might visualize my immune system as a team of vigilant guardians protecting my body, or imagine healing light permeating areas of discomfort.

Research suggests that visualization can influence physiological responses. Athletes often use mental rehearsal to enhance performance, and patients undergoing medical treatments may experience better outcomes when employing positive imagery. In my experience, visualization fosters a proactive mindset, empowering me to participate actively in my healing journey.

Positive Thinking and Affirmations

Cultivating a positive mindset is also crucial. **Positive thinking** doesn't mean ignoring challenges but rather approaching them with optimism and resilience. I practice affirmations—statements that reinforce constructive beliefs. For instance, repeating phrases like "My body is strong and capable of healing" reinforces a supportive inner dialogue.

This shift in mindset can reduce stress hormones like cortisol, which, when elevated chronically, can impair immune function. By fostering positivity, I create an internal environment conducive to healing.

Breathwork and Movement

Engaging in **breathwork** and mindful movement, such as **yoga** or **tai chi**, further connects the mind and body. Conscious breathing exercises help regulate the nervous system, promoting relaxation and reducing anxiety. Movement practices enhance body awareness and flexibility, supporting physical health while calming the mind.

Through these practices, I find a harmonious balance between activity and rest, exertion and relaxation. They remind me that healing is not just about the absence of illness but the presence of vitality and balance.

The Impact of Stress on Healing

CONSCIOUSNESS AND PERCEPTION

Understanding the detrimental effects of stress underscores the importance of conscious practices. Chronic stress can lead to a host of health issues, including cardiovascular disease, digestive problems, and weakened immunity. Stress triggers the "fight or flight" response, diverting energy away from healing and maintenance.

By employing mindfulness, meditation, and relaxation techniques, I mitigate the impact of stress. These practices activate the **parasympathetic nervous system**, promoting "rest and digest" functions that support healing. They help me navigate life's challenges with greater equanimity, reducing the physiological toll of stress.

Cultural Perspectives on Consciousness and Healing

Different cultures have long recognized the connection between consciousness and healing. Traditional Chinese Medicine (TCM), for example, emphasizes the flow of **Qi**—vital energy—throughout the body. Practices like acupuncture and Qigong aim to balance this energy, supporting health.

In Ayurveda, the ancient Indian system of medicine, consciousness is central to understanding health and disease. It advocates for a harmonious balance between mind, body, and spirit, employing meditation, herbal remedies, and dietary practices to restore equilibrium.

These traditions highlight the universal recognition of the mind-body connection. They offer valuable insights and techniques that enrich my own practices, reminding me that healing is a holistic process that transcends cultural boundaries.

Emotions and Physical Health

Emotions play a significant role in physical health. Negative emotions like anger, fear, and sadness can manifest as physical symptoms, while positive emotions like joy, love, and contentment can promote well-being.

I pay attention to my emotional states, acknowledging them without judgment. When I experience difficult emotions, I use mindfulness to observe them and explore their origins. This awareness prevents emotions from becoming suppressed or overwhelming, reducing their potential negative impact on my health.

Expressing emotions through journaling, art, or conversation provides an outlet and fosters emotional resilience. Connecting with others for support enhances feelings of belonging and reduces isolation, further supporting healing.

Belief, Expectation, and the Healing Journey

Our beliefs and expectations can significantly influence healing outcomes. The **nocebo effect**, the counterpart to the placebo effect, occurs when negative expectations lead to worse health outcomes. This phenomenon underscores the importance of cultivating hopeful and positive beliefs.

I strive to maintain realistic optimism. While acknowledging the reality of health challenges, I focus on possibilities for improvement and recovery. Setting positive intentions and visualizing desired outcomes reinforces a constructive mindset.

This approach doesn't guarantee specific results but creates a supportive psychological environment that can enhance the effectiveness of medical treatments. It empowers me to be an active participant in my healing journey.

Complementary Therapies Involving Consciousness

In addition to personal practices, I explore complementary therapies that engage consciousness in healing:

- **Biofeedback**: This technique involves using electronic devices to monitor physiological functions like heart rate or muscle tension. By receiving real-time feedback, I learn to control these functions consciously, reducing stress and promoting relaxation.
- **Hypnotherapy**: Guided hypnosis can access subconscious patterns and beliefs, facilitating behavioral changes and emotional healing. Under professional guidance, hypnotherapy helps me address underlying issues that may affect health.
- **Energy Healing**: Modalities like Reiki and Healing Touch focus on balancing the body's energy fields. While scientific evidence is limited, many people, including myself, find these practices enhance relaxation and well-being.
- **Art and Music Therapy**: Engaging in creative expression taps into subconscious processes, allowing for emotional release and insight. These therapies provide avenues for healing that transcend verbal communication.

The Role of Social Support and Connectedness

Human connections are vital to healing. Social support provides emotional comfort, practical assistance, and a sense of belonging. Sharing experiences with others who understand fosters empathy and reduces feelings of isolation.

I actively cultivate relationships with family, friends, and support groups. These connections not only uplift my spirits but also offer different perspectives and coping strategies. Participating in community activities or volunteering enhances my sense of purpose and contribution, which positively impacts mental health.

Scientific Research and Evidence

While personal experiences and traditional practices highlight the importance of consciousness in healing, scientific research provides additional support:

- **Mindfulness-Based Stress Reduction (MBSR)** programs have been shown to reduce symptoms of chronic pain, anxiety, and depression.
- Studies on **meditation** demonstrate changes in brain structure and function, associated with improved emotional regulation and cognitive abilities.
- Research on the **placebo effect** reveals that expectation and belief can activate neurotransmitters and endorphins, influencing pain perception and other physiological responses.

These findings reinforce the idea that consciousness and mental states can have measurable effects on physical health.

Addressing Criticisms and Limitations

It's important to approach the connection between consciousness and healing with a balanced perspective. While there is evidence supporting the mind-body link, not all claims are substantiated, and results can vary among individuals.

Some criticisms include:

- **Placebo and Nocebo Effects**: These phenomena illustrate the power of belief but also highlight that outcomes can be unpredictable and influenced by numerous factors.
- **Overemphasis on Positive Thinking**: While positivity can support healing, unrealistic expectations may lead to disappointment or self-blame if desired outcomes aren't achieved.
- **Alternative Therapies Lacking Evidence**: Not all complementary practices are supported by rigorous scientific studies. It's crucial to consider evidence and consult professionals when exploring new therapies.

I acknowledge these limitations and advocate for an integrative approach that combines evidence-based medicine with supportive conscious practices. Collaboration with healthcare providers ensures that treatments are appropriate and safe.

Personal Anecdotes and Experiences

In my own life, I've witnessed the impact of consciousness on healing. During times of illness, engaging in mindfulness and meditation has provided relief from anxiety and improved my overall well-being. Practicing visualization and affirmations has bolstered my confidence in recovery.

I've also seen loved ones benefit from these approaches. For example, a family member coping with chronic pain found that meditation and yoga significantly reduced their discomfort and reliance on medication.

These experiences reinforce my belief in the power of the mind-body connection. They inspire me to continue exploring and sharing these practices.

Philosophical Considerations

The relationship between consciousness and healing also invites philosophical reflection. Questions arise, such as:

- What is the nature of consciousness, and how does it interact with the physical body?
- Can we consider healing as not just a physical process but a holistic transformation involving mind, body, and spirit?
- How do cultural and personal beliefs shape our experiences of illness and recovery?

Contemplating these questions enriches my understanding and encourages a more nuanced approach to health. It emphasizes that healing is a deeply personal journey, influenced by individual perspectives and values.

Conclusion: Embracing a Holistic Approach to Healing

The exploration of consciousness and healing has led me to embrace a holistic approach that integrates physical, mental, and emotional well-being. Recognizing the interplay between mind and body empowers me to take an active role in my health.

By cultivating practices like mindfulness, meditation, positive thinking, and engaging with supportive communities, I enhance my capacity for healing. These practices do not replace medical treatments but complement them, addressing the whole person rather than just symptoms.

This approach fosters resilience, compassion, and a deeper connection to myself and others. It acknowledges that while we may not control all aspects of health, we can influence our experiences and responses.

As I continue this journey, I remain open to learning and adapting. Healing is an ongoing process, and consciousness is a dynamic force that can guide us toward greater well-being.

CONSCIOUSNESS AND PERCEPTION

Exercises and Reflections:

1. **Daily Mindfulness Practice:**
   - Set aside 15-20 minutes each day for mindfulness meditation. Focus on your breath, bodily sensations, or sounds around you. Observe thoughts and emotions as they arise, letting them pass without judgment.
2. **Healing Visualization:**
   - Create a detailed mental image of your body healing. Imagine cells regenerating, energy flowing smoothly, or light enveloping areas of discomfort. Engage all your senses to make the visualization vivid.
3. **Emotional Awareness Journal:**
   - Keep a journal to track your emotions and how they correlate with physical sensations. Reflect on patterns and consider ways to address negative emotions through conscious practices.
4. **Gratitude Practice:**
   - Each day, write down three things you are grateful for. This practice shifts focus toward positive aspects of life, promoting a hopeful mindset.
5. **Mindful Movement:**
   - Participate in yoga, tai chi, or qigong classes. These practices integrate movement with breath and awareness, enhancing the mind-body connection.
6. **Community Engagement:**
   - Join a support group or community organization related to health and wellness. Sharing experiences with others fosters connection and mutual support.

Chapter 16: Philosophy of Mind

The nature of consciousness and its relationship to the physical brain has been a central question in philosophy and science for centuries. This profound inquiry touches upon the essence of what it means to be human and challenges our understanding of reality itself. In my exploration of this intricate topic, I find myself aligning with a **dualistic** perspective—the belief that mind and body are distinct entities. The brain, in my view, attempts to comprehend consciousness, but consciousness itself transcends the physical processes of the brain.

The Dualistic Perspective: Mind and Body as Distinct Entities

Dualism posits that there are two fundamental kinds of substance: the physical (body) and the non-physical (mind). This viewpoint suggests that mental phenomena are non-physical and that the mind and body interact but are fundamentally different in nature.

My inclination toward dualism stems from several considerations:

1. **Subjective Experience (Qualia):** The unique, first-person experiences that each of us has—such as the redness of a sunset, the taste of vanilla, or the feeling of love—are deeply personal and subjective. These experiences, known as **qualia**, seem irreducible to mere physical processes. No matter how much we study the brain's workings, the subjective quality of experience remains elusive.
2. **Consciousness as Irreducible:** Consciousness doesn't seem to be something that can be fully explained by breaking it down into smaller physical components. While neurons and synapses can be studied, the emergence of awareness and self-reflection suggests a non-physical dimension.
3. **Intentionality:** Our thoughts often have aboutness—they are about something. This intentionality, the ability of the mind to refer to objects, ideas, or states beyond itself, doesn't have a clear counterpart in physical processes.
4. **Free Will:** The experience of making choices and exerting control over actions implies a conscious agent separate from deterministic physical laws. If the mind were purely physical, all actions would be

CONSCIOUSNESS AND PERCEPTION

predetermined by prior states, leaving no room for genuine choice.

The Brain's Role in Comprehending Consciousness

I see the brain as a sophisticated instrument that processes sensory information, facilitates movement, and enables communication. It serves as a mediator between the non-physical mind and the physical world. The brain attempts to comprehend consciousness by interpreting and organizing sensory inputs, memories, and thoughts. However, it doesn't generate consciousness itself; rather, it provides the means for consciousness to interact with the material realm.

This perspective can be likened to a pianist (the mind) playing a piano (the brain). The music produced depends on both the skill of the pianist and the quality of the piano. Damage to the piano affects the music, but it doesn't eliminate the pianist's ability to create music. Similarly, impairments to the brain can affect consciousness's expression without negating its existence.

Philosophical Foundations of Dualism

The dualistic view has a rich philosophical heritage:

- **René Descartes (1596–1650):** Often considered the father of modern dualism, Descartes posited that the mind and body are fundamentally different substances. His famous assertion, "Cogito, ergo sum" ("I think, therefore I am"), emphasizes the certainty of the mind's existence over the physical body's.
- **Plato (428–348 BCE):** Plato believed in the existence of an immortal soul separate from the physical body. He viewed the body as a temporary vessel for the soul, which possesses true knowledge and understanding.
- **Thomas Nagel's "What Is It Like to Be a Bat?":** Nagel argues that subjective experience cannot be fully captured by objective, physical explanations. There is something it is like to be a conscious creature that escapes reduction to physical terms.

These philosophical arguments reinforce the notion that consciousness possesses qualities that are fundamentally different from physical matter.

Challenges to Dualism: The Interaction Problem

Despite its compelling aspects, dualism faces significant challenges, the most notable being the **interaction problem**:

- **Causal Interaction:** If mind and body are separate substances, how do they interact causally? How can a non-physical mind influence a physical body, and vice versa? This question has puzzled philosophers for centuries.
- **Physical Conservation Laws:** The conservation of energy principle suggests that all physical events have physical causes. Introducing non-physical causes seems to violate this principle, leading to inconsistencies with established scientific laws.

- **Empirical Evidence:** Advances in neuroscience have demonstrated strong correlations between brain states and mental states. Brain injuries, chemical imbalances, and electrical stimulation can significantly alter consciousness, suggesting a closer link between mind and brain than dualism accounts for.

Physicalism: Consciousness as an Emergent Property

In contrast to dualism, **physicalism** (or materialism) holds that everything about the mind can be explained in physical terms. Consciousness arises from complex interactions within the brain's neural networks.

- **Neuroscientific Evidence:** Functional magnetic resonance imaging (fMRI) and other technologies have mapped brain activity corresponding to specific thoughts, emotions, and behaviors. This suggests that mental states are directly tied to physical brain states.
- **Eliminative Materialism:** Some physicalists argue that common-sense mental concepts (like beliefs and desires) will eventually be eliminated in favor of neuroscientific explanations, much like how science replaced concepts like "phlogiston" with oxygen in explaining combustion.
- **Artificial Intelligence:** The development of AI raises questions about consciousness emerging from complex information processing. If machines can exhibit behaviors akin to consciousness, it challenges the notion that consciousness requires a non-physical substance.

Why I Favor Dualism Despite Physicalist Arguments

While I acknowledge the strength of physicalist arguments and the importance of neuroscientific findings, I maintain a dualistic stance for several reasons:

1. **Incomplete Explanations:** Physical explanations often account for the mechanisms underlying mental processes but fail to capture the essence of subjective experience.
2. **The Hard Problem of Consciousness:** As David Chalmers highlights, explaining why and how physical processes give rise to conscious experience remains unsolved. Physicalism addresses the "easy problems" (like information processing) but not the hard problem.
3. **Irreducibility of Qualia:** The subjective quality of experiences resists reduction to objective, third-person descriptions.
4. **Personal Experiences:** Moments of introspection, creativity, and transcendence suggest to me that consciousness operates beyond physical constraints.

CONSCIOUSNESS AND PERCEPTION

Alternative Theories Bridging Mind and Matter

Recognizing the limitations of both dualism and physicalism, I explore alternative theories that attempt to bridge the gap:

- **Property Dualism:** Suggests that while there is only one kind of substance (physical), it possesses both physical and mental properties. Consciousness is seen as a property that emerges from physical systems but is not reducible to them.
- **Panpsychism:** Proposes that consciousness is a fundamental feature of the universe, present at all levels. Even elementary particles possess rudimentary forms of consciousness. This view offers a continuum between matter and mind.
- **Neutral Monism:** Asserts that there is a single, neutral substance underlying both mind and matter. Mental and physical states are two aspects of the same underlying reality.

These theories attempt to reconcile the subjective nature of consciousness with the objective findings of science, offering a more integrated understanding.

Implications of Dualism for Personal Identity

Dualism has significant implications for concepts like personal identity and the self:

- **Survival After Death:** If the mind is non-physical, it raises the possibility of consciousness existing independently of the body, suggesting potential for an afterlife or reincarnation.
- **Moral Responsibility:** Viewing the mind as separate from deterministic physical processes supports the notion of free will, reinforcing accountability for one's actions.
- **Mindfulness and Spiritual Practices:** Many spiritual traditions align with dualistic concepts, emphasizing the cultivation of the mind or soul as distinct from the body. Practices like meditation aim to transcend physical limitations and access deeper levels of consciousness.

Critiques and Counterarguments

Despite my inclination toward dualism, I recognize the importance of addressing critiques:

- **Neuroscientific Findings:** Conditions like Alzheimer's disease, brain injuries, and psychoactive substances clearly affect consciousness. This suggests a strong dependency of the mind on the physical brain.
    - **Response:** While the brain may influence the expression of consciousness, it doesn't necessarily generate it. Damage to the brain could impair the mind's ability to interact with the physical world without negating its separate existence.
- **Occam's Razor:** Introducing a non-physical mind adds complexity without empirical evidence.
    - **Response:** The inability of physicalism to fully explain subjective experience justifies exploring

alternative explanations, even if they are more complex.

Consciousness Studies and Future Directions

The study of consciousness is an evolving field, incorporating insights from neuroscience, psychology, philosophy, and quantum physics.

- **Integrated Information Theory (IIT):** Proposes that consciousness corresponds to the ability of a system to integrate information. While rooted in physical processes, IIT attempts to quantify consciousness, bridging subjective experience with objective measures.
- **Quantum Theories of Consciousness:** Some theorists suggest that quantum processes in the brain contribute to consciousness. While speculative, these ideas explore the possibility that consciousness arises from fundamental aspects of reality not yet fully understood.
- **Interdisciplinary Approaches:** Combining philosophy with empirical research may yield new insights. Acknowledging the limitations of current models encourages openness to novel theories.

Personal Reflections and Experiences

My personal journey informs my philosophical stance:

- **Moments of Transcendence:** Experiences during meditation, creative endeavors, or moments of profound connection have felt as though they originate beyond the physical self.
- **Intuitive Understanding:** There's an intuitive sense that my consciousness is more than the sum of neural processes—a feeling of continuity and depth that physical explanations don't capture.
- **Ethical Considerations:** Believing in a non-physical mind fosters a sense of responsibility and interconnectedness. It encourages me to consider the impact of my actions on a deeper level.

The Ongoing Mystery of Consciousness

Ultimately, consciousness remains one of the greatest mysteries. Whether one adopts a dualistic, physicalist, or alternative perspective, each offers valuable insights and faces challenges.

- **Embracing Uncertainty:** I accept that my understanding is incomplete. The complexity of consciousness may require new paradigms or ways of thinking.
- **The Role of Philosophy:** Philosophical inquiry remains vital in probing questions that science alone cannot answer. It encourages critical thinking and the exploration of ideas beyond empirical observation.
- **Interconnectedness of Mind and World:** Regardless of the mind's nature, our experiences shape our reality. How we perceive, interpret, and respond to the world influences our existence.

Conclusion: A Personal Synthesis

CONSCIOUSNESS AND PERCEPTION

My alignment with dualism reflects a belief in the richness and depth of consciousness—a dimension that transcends physical explanations. While acknowledging the challenges and the contributions of physicalism, I find that a dualistic perspective resonates with my experiences and intuitions.

The exploration of the philosophy of mind is not merely an academic exercise but a deeply personal journey. It shapes how I understand myself, relate to others, and find meaning in life. By remaining open to diverse perspectives and embracing the mystery of consciousness, I continue to seek a deeper understanding of the mind's true nature.

Exercises and Reflections:

1. **Mind-Body Journaling:**
   - Reflect on experiences where your mental state seemed to influence your physical state (e.g., stress affecting health). Consider how this relates to the mind-body connection.
2. **Thought Experiment:**
   - Imagine a scenario where your consciousness exists independently of your physical body. How would this change your perception of self and identity?
3. **Philosophical Dialogue:**
   - Engage with writings from both dualist and physicalist philosophers. Note points of agreement and contention. How do these arguments align or conflict with your own views?
4. **Meditation on Consciousness:**
   - Practice mindfulness meditation, focusing on the nature of awareness itself. Observe thoughts and sensations without attachment. Reflect on whether consciousness feels separate from or intertwined with the physical body.

Chapter 17: Consciousness in Eastern Philosophies

The exploration of consciousness has been a central theme in Eastern philosophies for millennia. Traditions such as Buddhism, Hinduism, and Taoism offer profound insights into the nature of the mind, the self, and reality. My personal journey has been deeply influenced by the practices and teachings of Buddhism and Hinduism. Engaging in the art of meditation in Buddhism and participating in prayer and rituals in Hinduism have helped me transcend ordinary consciousness, opening pathways to deeper understanding and awareness.

The Art of Meditation in Buddhism

My introduction to Buddhism began with the practice of **meditation**, a foundational element in the pursuit of enlightenment. Meditation in Buddhism is not merely a relaxation technique but a disciplined practice aimed at understanding the true nature of reality and the self.

Mindfulness Meditation (Vipassana)

One of the first techniques I learned was **Vipassana**, or insight meditation. This practice involves cultivating mindfulness by observing thoughts, sensations, and emotions as they arise and pass away. By focusing on the breath and maintaining a non-judgmental awareness, I began to notice the impermanent and interconnected nature of all experiences.

Through regular Vipassana meditation, I experienced a heightened sense of presence. I became more attuned to the subtle fluctuations of my mind, recognizing patterns of thought that contributed to stress or dissatisfaction. This awareness allowed me to detach from these patterns, reducing their impact on my well-being.

Loving-Kindness Meditation (Metta)

Another significant practice was **Metta** meditation, which focuses on cultivating unconditional love and compassion toward oneself and others. By repeating phrases like "May I be happy, may I be healthy, may I be at peace," and extending these wishes to all beings, I fostered a sense of connection and empathy.

CONSCIOUSNESS AND PERCEPTION

This practice transformed my relationships, both with myself and others. It softened feelings of anger or resentment and encouraged a more compassionate approach to conflicts. I found that as I cultivated loving-kindness, my sense of isolation diminished, and a deeper understanding of interconnectedness emerged.

The Four Noble Truths and the Eightfold Path

Buddhist philosophy provided a framework for understanding suffering and the path to liberation. The **Four Noble Truths** taught me that suffering is an inherent part of life, arising from attachment and desire. By recognizing the causes of suffering, I could begin to address them.

The **Eightfold Path** offered practical guidelines for ethical living, mental discipline, and wisdom. Practices like right mindfulness and right concentration reinforced my meditation efforts, while right action and right speech guided my interactions with others.

Embracing these teachings helped me navigate life's challenges with greater equanimity. I learned to accept impermanence and to let go of clinging to transient experiences, leading to a more balanced and peaceful state of mind.

Prayer and Rituals in Hinduism

My exploration of Hinduism introduced me to a rich tapestry of beliefs, rituals, and practices aimed at understanding the self and its relationship to the divine. Hinduism's emphasis on the inner journey and the realization of one's true nature resonated deeply with me.

Bhakti Yoga: The Path of Devotion

One of the key practices I embraced was **Bhakti Yoga**, the path of devotion. Through prayer, chanting, and worship, I sought to cultivate a personal relationship with the divine. Engaging in rituals at temples and at home created a sense of reverence and connection.

Chanting sacred mantras, such as the **Gayatri Mantra** or the **Maha Mrityunjaya Mantra**, became a daily practice. The vibrations of the sounds and the focus on the words facilitated a meditative state, calming the mind and opening the heart.

Bhakti Yoga taught me the value of surrender and humility. By recognizing a higher power and offering my actions and intentions to it, I found a sense of purpose and alignment. This devotion transcended religious labels, fostering a universal appreciation for the sacredness of life.

Jnana Yoga: The Path of Knowledge

In addition to devotional practices, I explored **Jnana Yoga**, the path of knowledge. This involved studying sacred texts like the **Upanishads**, the **Bhagavad Gita**, and the **Vedas**. These scriptures delve into profound philosophical concepts about the nature of reality, the self (Atman), and the ultimate reality (Brahman).

Through contemplation and self-inquiry, I questioned the nature of my identity. The teachings suggested that the true self is not the body or the mind but the eternal, unchanging consciousness underlying all existence. This realization challenged my conventional perceptions and encouraged a shift toward a more expansive sense of self.

Karma Yoga: The Path of Selfless Action

Karma Yoga emphasized the importance of selfless service. By performing actions without attachment to the results, I practiced letting go of ego-driven motivations. Engaging in volunteer work and helping others became an expression of this principle.

This approach to action fostered a sense of unity and compassion. It reduced stress associated with expectations and outcomes, allowing me to act with sincerity and integrity. Karma Yoga reinforced the interconnectedness of all beings and the impact of our actions on the greater whole.

Transcending Consciousness Through Belief and Zen

While Zen is a school of Mahayana Buddhism originating in China and Japan, its emphasis on direct experience and meditation influenced my practices. The integration of **belief** and **Zen** provided pathways to transcend ordinary consciousness.

Zen Meditation (Zazen)

Zazen, or seated meditation, focuses on just sitting without specific goals or attachments. This practice emphasizes being fully present and aware, allowing thoughts and sensations to arise and pass without engagement.

Through Zazen, I experienced moments of profound stillness and clarity. The practice taught me to embrace simplicity and to find depth in the mundane. It challenged habitual thinking patterns and opened space for intuitive insights.

Koan Study

CONSCIOUSNESS AND PERCEPTION

Zen often employs **koans**, paradoxical questions or statements that defy logical analysis. Pondering koans like "What is the sound of one hand clapping?" disrupted conventional thought processes and prompted direct realization.

Engaging with koans sharpened my awareness and highlighted the limitations of rational thinking. It encouraged me to access deeper layers of understanding beyond intellect, tapping into intuitive wisdom.

Integration of Belief

Belief played a crucial role in my journey. Embracing the teachings with sincerity allowed me to fully engage with the practices. Belief provided a foundation of trust and openness, creating a receptive state for transformation.

At the same time, these traditions encouraged questioning and personal exploration. The balance between belief and inquiry ensured that my understanding was authentic and experiential rather than dogmatic.

Influence on Perception of Self and Reality

These practices and teachings profoundly influenced my perception of self and reality.

Dissolution of the Ego

Through meditation and self-inquiry, I recognized the constructed nature of the ego—the sense of a separate self defined by thoughts, roles, and identities. By observing the transient nature of thoughts and emotions, I began to disidentify from them.

This realization led to a sense of liberation. Without the constraints of a fixed ego, I experienced greater flexibility and openness. It reduced suffering associated with clinging to self-image and allowed for more authentic interactions.

Interconnectedness

Both Buddhism and Hinduism emphasize the interconnectedness of all beings. Understanding concepts like **dependent origination** in Buddhism and the **unity of Atman and Brahman** in Hinduism fostered a sense of oneness with the universe.

This perspective shifted how I related to others and the environment. Compassion became a natural response, arising from the recognition that harming others ultimately harms oneself. It inspired actions aligned with the well-being of the whole.

Impermanence and Acceptance

Embracing the impermanent nature of phenomena encouraged acceptance of change and loss. Recognizing that all experiences are transient reduced anxiety about the future and attachment to the past.

This acceptance cultivated peace and presence. It allowed me to engage fully with each moment, appreciating its uniqueness without grasping or aversion.

Practical Applications in Daily Life

Integrating these philosophies into daily life enriched my experiences and relationships.

Mindful Living

Applying mindfulness beyond formal meditation, I practiced being fully present in everyday activities—eating, walking, listening. This heightened awareness enhanced enjoyment and reduced stress.

Mindful communication improved relationships. By listening attentively and responding thoughtfully, interactions became more meaningful and empathetic.

Ethical Conduct

The moral guidelines in both traditions—such as the **Five Precepts** in Buddhism and the concept of **Dharma** in Hinduism—guided my actions toward integrity and responsibility.

Avoiding harm, speaking truthfully, and acting generously fostered trust and harmony. Ethical conduct became a reflection of inner values rather than external obligations.

Service and Compassion

Engaging in community service and acts of kindness embodied the principles of compassion and selflessness. Volunteering at shelters, supporting environmental initiatives, or simply offering a helping hand reinforced the interconnectedness I experienced.

These actions not only benefited others but also enriched my own sense of purpose and fulfillment.

Challenges and Growth

The journey was not without challenges. Confronting deeply ingrained habits and beliefs required patience and perseverance.

Overcoming Resistance

CONSCIOUSNESS AND PERCEPTION

At times, meditation brought up uncomfortable emotions or restlessness. Staying with these experiences without judgment taught me resilience and acceptance.

Balancing Traditions

Navigating different philosophies required discernment. While there are commonalities, Buddhism and Hinduism have distinct teachings. Integrating them respectfully meant understanding the context and essence of each.

Maintaining Consistency

Establishing regular practice amidst daily responsibilities demanded commitment. Creating routines and prioritizing spiritual growth helped sustain progress.

Reflections on Consciousness

Engaging with Eastern philosophies expanded my understanding of consciousness.

Consciousness as Fundamental

These traditions often view consciousness not merely as a byproduct of the brain but as a fundamental aspect of reality. In Hinduism, **Brahman** is the ultimate reality, pure consciousness from which everything emanates.

This perspective aligns with my inclination toward seeing consciousness as intrinsic to the universe, as explored in earlier chapters.

States of Consciousness

Practices led to experiences of altered states of consciousness—deep meditation, heightened awareness, or moments of unity. These states provided glimpses into the vast potential of the mind.

Self-Realization

The ultimate goal in these traditions is often self-realization or enlightenment—awakening to one's true nature beyond ego and illusion. While this is an ongoing journey, the practices have brought me closer to understanding and embodying this realization.

Integration with Western Perspectives

Bridging Eastern philosophies with Western thought enriched my exploration.

Complementary Insights

Western philosophy and science often focus on analytical and empirical approaches, while Eastern traditions emphasize experiential wisdom. Integrating both offers a holistic understanding.

For example, mindfulness practices have been incorporated into psychology, enhancing therapeutic approaches for mental health.

Cultural Sensitivity

Respecting the origins and contexts of these philosophies is essential. Avoiding cultural appropriation and honoring the traditions ensure ethical engagement.

Conclusion

The teachings and practices of Buddhism and Hinduism have profoundly shaped my understanding of consciousness and reality. Through meditation, prayer, rituals, and philosophical inquiry, I have experienced transformative shifts in perception and being.

These traditions offer timeless wisdom relevant to contemporary life. They provide tools for personal growth, ethical living, and deep connection with oneself and the universe.

My journey continues as I delve deeper into these teachings, integrating their insights into daily life and sharing their benefits with others.

Chapter 18: Creativity and Consciousness

The interplay between creativity and consciousness has long fascinated philosophers, artists, and thinkers throughout history. Creativity, the ability to produce something new and valuable, is often seen as a manifestation of consciousness—a means by which the mind expresses ideas, emotions, and visions that transcend ordinary perception. In my experience, consciousness plays a pivotal role in dictating the mood and tempo of creativity. Higher levels of consciousness enhance creativity by aligning us with deeper insights and understandings, often connected to the divine or universal mind. This connection manifests in my life through an understanding of what the divine embodies and how that understanding fuels the creative process.

Consciousness can be viewed as the awareness of internal and external existence, encompassing thoughts, feelings, sensations, and perceptions. It is the lens through which we interpret and interact with the world. Creativity, on the other hand, is not merely the production of art or innovation; it is a fundamental aspect of human expression, a reflection of our inner selves projected into the external world. The relationship between consciousness and creativity is profound and multifaceted. Consciousness acts as a catalyst for creativity, expanding the mind to new possibilities and breaking free from conventional patterns of thinking. It allows for the synthesis of disparate ideas, leading to novel creations that resonate on a deeper level.

In my journey, I have found that consciousness dictates the mood and tempo for creativity by influencing my emotional and mental states. The mood sets the emotional tone, while the tempo refers to the pace at which creative ideas flow. Positive emotions such as joy, love, and curiosity foster openness and exploration, enhancing creativity by encouraging a free flow of ideas. Conversely, even challenging emotions like sadness or frustration can inspire profound creative expressions by tapping into deep feelings that demand to be articulated. Mental clarity is equally essential. A clear and focused mind facilitates the flow of creative ideas, and practices that enhance mindfulness and presence can significantly improve mental clarity. When consciousness aligns with the creative process, I often enter a "flow state"—a state of complete immersion and enjoyment in the activity where time seems to fade, and creativity flows effortlessly.

Higher levels of consciousness involve heightened awareness, expanded perceptions, and a deeper understanding of oneself and the universe. Elevating consciousness enhances creativity in several ways. It grants access to intuitive knowledge that goes beyond rational thought. This intuition can guide creative endeavors, leading to innovative ideas and solutions that might not emerge through analytical thinking alone. I believe that higher consciousness connects us to a universal source of wisdom or the divine. This connection inspires creativity that feels transcendent, as if tapping into a wellspring of inspiration that flows through us rather than originating solely within us. It is a feeling of being a conduit for creative energy that originates from a higher plane.

Understanding what the divine embodies has been instrumental in my creative process. The divine, in this context, represents the ultimate source of creation, wisdom, and love. By aligning my consciousness with this source, I feel that I become a co-creator, channeling inspiration into tangible forms. This alignment imbues my creative acts with deeper meaning and purpose, transforming creativity from a personal endeavor into a contribution to a greater whole. It elevates the act of creation to a sacred practice, one that honors the divine spark within and seeks to express universal truths.

Meditation has been a cornerstone in elevating my consciousness and enhancing creativity. Regular meditation quiets mental chatter, creating space for new ideas to emerge. By focusing inward and cultivating stillness, I access deeper layers of thought and feeling. Meditation heightens awareness, allowing me to become more attuned to subtle thoughts and emotions that provide rich material for creative exploration. Visualization techniques practiced during meditation enable me to imagine creative outcomes vividly, bridging the gap between ideas and their realization. By visualizing the creative process and the desired outcome, I set a clear intention that guides my actions and aligns them with higher consciousness.

Dream journaling is another practice that has significantly influenced my creativity. Dreams provide a window into the subconscious mind, revealing symbolic messages and insights that can inspire creative projects. By recording and reflecting on my dreams, I uncover hidden desires, fears, and ideas that fuel creativity. The subconscious often communicates in symbols and narratives

CONSCIOUSNESS AND PERCEPTION

that, when interpreted, can lead to profound revelations and innovative concepts.

Engaging with nature serves as a profound source of inspiration and a means to elevate consciousness. Immersing myself in natural settings connects me to the rhythms and patterns of the earth. Observing the intricate details of a leaf, the flow of a river, or the expanse of the sky fosters a sense of wonder and unity with the natural world. This connection enhances my creativity by providing fresh perspectives and reminding me of the interconnectedness of all things. Nature's effortless creativity—the way it continually evolves and adapts—inspires me to embrace fluidity and spontaneity in my own creative endeavours.

Approaching artistic expression as a spiritual practice has deepened both my creative process and the outcomes. By setting clear intentions before beginning a creative task, I align my work with higher purposes. This might involve dedicating the work to a specific cause, emotion, or aspect of the divine. Creating a sacred space for creativity, whether it's a physical space adorned with inspiring objects or a mental space cultivated through ritual, elevates the atmosphere and honors the creative process. Incorporating rituals such as lighting candles, burning incense, or playing music can enhance focus and invite a sense of reverence.

Allowing ideas to flow rather than forcing them respects the natural ebb and flow of creativity. I've learned that creativity cannot be compelled; it flourishes in an environment of openness and acceptance. This approach reduces pressure and anxiety associated with creative blocks, fostering a more joyful and authentic expression. It's about trusting the process and being receptive to inspiration when it arises.

Understanding what the divine embodies has guided me in recognizing that creation is an ongoing process. The universe is in a constant state of becoming, and by participating in creative acts, I contribute to this continual unfolding. Embracing paradoxes, such as the coexistence of order and chaos, certainty and mystery, allows for more nuanced and profound creative expressions. It encourages me to explore themes that challenge conventional wisdom and to appreciate the complexity of existence.

Creativity is also a collective experience, influenced by and contributing to the collective consciousness. Cultural influences shape creative expression by providing context, symbols, and narratives that resonate with shared experiences. Engaging with cultural arts expands creative perspectives, exposing me to diverse forms and ideas that enrich my own work. Collaborative creativity, working with others, combines different consciousness levels, leading to richer and more complex creative outcomes. It fosters a sense of community and shared purpose, enhancing the impact of the creative endeavour.

Participating in global consciousness movements, such as environmental initiatives or social justice campaigns, inspires creativity with purpose. Aligning creative work with causes that aim to elevate global consciousness infuses it with meaning and urgency. It transforms personal expression into a vehicle for change, amplifying its significance and reach.

Challenges inevitably arise in the creative process, even when consciousness is elevated. Creative blocks can stem from fear, self-doubt, or overthinking, hindering the free flow of ideas. Practices that elevate consciousness, such as meditation and mindfulness, help dissolve these blocks by fostering a non-judgmental awareness of thoughts and feelings. Recognizing and addressing ego interference is crucial. The ego may impose limitations or seek control over the creative process, leading to rigidity or resistance. Cultivating self-awareness reduces ego influence, allowing for more authentic and uninhibited expression.

Balancing structure and flow is another essential aspect. Creativity thrives on both discipline and spontaneity. Establishing routines and setting goals provide a framework within which creativity can flourish, while remaining open to improvisation and unexpected inspirations keeps the process dynamic and alive. Consciousness practices help maintain this balance by promoting flexibility and adaptability.

Techniques to elevate consciousness specifically for enhancing creativity include breathwork, movement practices, journaling, and artistic exploration. Breathwork, such as pranayama or conscious breathing, regulates energy flow and calms the mind, increasing presence and connection to the body. Movement practices like yoga, tai chi, or dance harmonize the body and mind, opening channels for creative energy and allowing expressive release.

Journaling and free writing tap into subconscious thoughts and feelings, providing a rich source of material for creative endeavours. Stream-of-consciousness writing, where thoughts are recorded uncensored, can uncover ideas and connections that might otherwise remain hidden. Reflective journaling deepens the understanding of personal experiences and emotions, informing and enriching creative work.

Artistic exploration without specific goals encourages experimentation and play. Trying new mediums or techniques expands creative horizons and breaks habitual patterns. This openness to discovery fosters innovation and keeps the creative process engaging and enjoyable.

Engaging with symbolism and archetypes enhances creativity by connecting with universal themes and narratives. Studying mythology and exploring personal symbols provide rich material for creative inspiration. These symbols tap into collective unconsciousness, resonating with others on a deep level and adding layers of meaning to creative works.

Creativity also serves as a path to higher consciousness. Engaging in creative activities fosters self-exploration and personal growth. It encourages us to confront and express our innermost thoughts and feelings, facilitating healing and integration. Immersion in the creative process can lead to transcendent experiences where the sense of self expands beyond ordinary boundaries. These moments of flow and connection elevate consciousness, contributing to a deeper understanding of oneself and the world.

Integrating creativity and consciousness into daily life enhances overall well-being and fulfilment. Mindful living, bringing awareness to routine tasks, enhances appreciation and may spark creative ideas. Cultivating curiosity uncovers inspiration in unexpected places, keeping the mind engaged and receptive. Balancing input and output is essential. Consuming inspiring content through reading, listening to music, or viewing art enriches the creative reservoir, while allowing time for rest and reflection nurtures the mind and prevents burnout.

Community engagement amplifies the impact of creativity and consciousness practices. Sharing creative work with others fosters connection and mutual inspiration. Supporting others' creativity elevates collective consciousness, contributing to a more vibrant and empathetic society. Collaborative projects blend different perspectives and consciousness levels, leading to innovative and meaningful outcomes.

Reflecting on my journey, embracing the connection between consciousness and creativity has transformed my approach to both. Creativity becomes more fulfilling when aligned with higher consciousness, as it resonates with deeper values and purposes. It becomes a means of personal expression and a contribution to the greater good. The journey is ongoing; as consciousness expands, so does creative potential. Each new insight or experience opens doors to further exploration and expression.

Understanding that creativity is a profound expression of consciousness, a bridge between the inner world and external reality, enriches the creative process. By nurturing consciousness, we unlock greater creative abilities, accessing insights that may otherwise remain dormant. Connecting with a higher purpose or the divine infuses creativity with meaning and impact, transforming it into a force for personal and collective evolution.

In conclusion, the symbiotic relationship between creativity and consciousness offers a path toward personal fulfilment and collective growth. By elevating consciousness, we enhance our creative potentials, accessing deeper insights and inspirations. Engaging in practices that nurture both consciousness and creativity enriches our lives and contributes positively to the world around us. It is a journey of discovery, a dance between the seen and unseen, reflecting the infinite possibilities within us and the divine spark that animates all creation.

Chapter 19: Death, Dying, and Consciousness

Death has been a subject of contemplation and mystery since the dawn of human consciousness. It is the inevitable destination that awaits all living beings, yet its true nature remains elusive. Throughout my life, I have pondered the essence of death and what it means for consciousness. I believe that consciousness transcends somewhere or someplace after death. To me, death is not merely an end but a continuation or transition into another state of existence. However, I also acknowledge that it can be perceived as an end, depending on where the soul journeys to. This chapter delves deep into my reflections on death, dying, and the journey of consciousness beyond the physical realm.

Consciousness, in my understanding, is more than just the byproduct of neural activity in the brain. It is the essence of our being—the soul or spirit that animates the physical body. When the body ceases to function, I believe that consciousness does not simply vanish but transcends to another plane of existence. This belief is rooted in several considerations, both philosophical and experiential.

Firstly, the law of conservation of energy in physics states that energy cannot be created or destroyed but only transformed from one form to another. If we consider consciousness as a form of energy or a manifestation of energy, it stands to reason that it continues in some form after death. This perspective suggests that death is a transformation rather than a cessation.

Secondly, numerous accounts of near-death experiences (NDEs) have intrigued me. Individuals who have been clinically dead and then revived often report experiences that suggest a continuation of consciousness independent of the physical body. These experiences commonly include sensations of floating above one's body, moving through a tunnel toward a bright light, encountering deceased loved ones, or feeling an overwhelming sense of peace and unconditional love. While skeptics may attribute these experiences to physiological or psychological processes during trauma, the consistency and profound impact of NDEs across cultures and ages suggest that there may be more to explore regarding consciousness beyond physical life.

Thirdly, the phenomena of reincarnation and past-life memories provide compelling anecdotes for the continuation of consciousness. There are documented cases, particularly among young children, who recall specific details of previous lives that they could not have known through ordinary means. Investigations into these claims have sometimes validated the details provided, further fueling the debate about the soul's journey beyond a single lifetime.

Spiritual and religious teachings from various cultures offer rich narratives about the afterlife, the soul's journey, and the nature of consciousness after death. Many traditions, such as Hinduism and Buddhism, espouse the concept of samsara—the cycle of birth, death, and rebirth—where the soul evolves through successive incarnations based on karma. In these beliefs, death is a transition, a necessary step in the soul's ongoing journey toward enlightenment or liberation.

Viewing death as a transition or continuation offers a perspective that diminishes the fear and finality often associated with it. If consciousness persists beyond physical demise, then death becomes a passage to another state of being rather than an absolute end. This viewpoint aligns with the metaphor of life as a journey, where death is merely a change in scenery or a new chapter in an ongoing story. It invites a broader understanding of existence, one that encompasses multiple dimensions or planes of reality.

In this context, death can be seen as a new beginning. It may mark the end of a physical existence but the commencement of a new journey for the soul. This could involve entering a spiritual realm, reincarnating into a new life, or merging with a universal consciousness. The transformation analogy is apt here; just as a caterpillar undergoes metamorphosis to become a butterfly, shedding its former self to embrace a new form, death could represent a transformative process for consciousness. This perspective imbues life with purpose and continuity, suggesting that our actions and experiences contribute to a larger tapestry of growth and evolution.

However, I also acknowledge that death can be perceived as an end, depending on one's philosophical or scientific standpoint. From a strictly materialist perspective, consciousness is a product of brain activity, and when the brain ceases to function, consciousness extinguishes. This view holds that death marks the absolute end of existence for the individual, with no

CONSCIOUSNESS AND PERCEPTION

continuation beyond the physical. Some may find this perspective bleak, while others may see it as a call to cherish the finite nature of life and make the most of the time we have.

Recognizing the possibility of death as an end adds depth to the contemplation of mortality. It encourages a balanced approach, where one can appreciate life fully without taking the present moment for granted. It also fosters empathy and understanding toward diverse beliefs about death and the afterlife, acknowledging that this mystery has been approached in myriad ways across cultures and eras.

My personal experiences have significantly shaped my beliefs about death and consciousness. Encounters with loss, such as the passing of loved ones, have prompted deep introspection. Observing the stillness of a body once vibrant with life, I felt that something essential—the consciousness or soul—had departed. This absence reinforced my sense that consciousness is not merely a physical phenomenon but something that transcends the material form.

Meditative practices have also influenced my perspective. Through meditation, I have experienced moments that suggest consciousness extends beyond the physical self. These include feelings of unity with the universe, encounters with inner light, and sensations of timelessness. Such experiences reinforce my belief in a transcendent consciousness that is not confined to the boundaries of the physical body.

Occasionally, I have noticed synchronicities or meaningful coincidences that seem to connect me with those who have passed on. These signs, whether through dreams, unexpected encounters, or intuitive feelings, hint at the possibility of continued existence and communication beyond death. While such experiences are subjective, they contribute to my personal understanding of consciousness and its potential to transcend physical demise.

Exploring various cultural and philosophical perspectives has further enriched my understanding. Eastern philosophies, such as Hinduism and Buddhism, offer comprehensive frameworks about death and the soul's journey. Hinduism teaches the concept of the Atman (soul) being eternal and undergoing cycles of rebirth until achieving moksha—liberation from the cycle of birth and death. Buddhism emphasizes the impermanence of all phenomena, including the self, and views death as a transition in the ongoing process of samsara, influenced by karma and leading toward enlightenment.

Western philosophies have also grappled with the nature of death and consciousness. Ancient Greek thinkers like Plato posited the immortality of the soul, suggesting that it exists before birth and continues after death. In modern times, some philosophers and scientists have explored the idea of consciousness as a fundamental aspect of the universe, potentially surviving physical death. The field of consciousness studies has expanded to include interdisciplinary approaches that consider quantum physics, neuroscience, and metaphysics.

Near-death experiences provide intriguing insights into the possibility of consciousness beyond death. Reports of NDEs often include common elements such as out-of-body experiences, encounters with a bright light or spiritual beings, life reviews, and profound feelings of peace and unconditional love. While some researchers attribute these phenomena to neurological or chemical processes in the brain during extreme stress, others argue that NDEs offer evidence of consciousness existing independently of the physical body.

Quantum physics introduces concepts that challenge conventional notions of reality and may have implications for understanding consciousness. The phenomenon of quantum entanglement, where particles remain connected such that the state of one instantly influences the state of another regardless of distance, suggests a level of interconnectedness that transcends physical space. Some theorists propose that consciousness itself may be a fundamental component of the universe, not confined to the brain but part of a larger, non-local reality. While these ideas are speculative and require further exploration, they open avenues for considering how consciousness might persist beyond physical death.

The concept of the soul's journey encompasses various paths that consciousness may take after death. Reincarnation, as believed in certain traditions, posits that the soul is reborn into new lives, continuing to learn and evolve through different experiences. Ascension theories suggest that the soul progresses to higher planes of existence or spiritual realms, advancing toward ultimate unity with the divine. Other beliefs hold that consciousness may merge with a universal essence, transcending individual identity and becoming part of the collective consciousness.

Beliefs about death and consciousness have profound ethical and existential implications. Viewing life as part of a larger journey imbues actions with purpose and responsibility. It encourages personal growth, compassion, and ethical living, as one's choices may influence not only this life but future existences or states of being. Understanding death as a transition can alleviate fear and anxiety, allowing for a more peaceful acceptance of mortality. It shifts the focus from fear of the unknown to curiosity and openness about the possibilities that lie beyond.

Grief and healing processes are also influenced by beliefs about the continuation of consciousness. Feeling that loved ones continue to exist in some form can provide comfort and a sense of ongoing relationship. Rituals that honor the deceased acknowledge their continued influence and presence in our lives. Accepting death as a natural part of existence aids in processing loss and finding peace, recognizing that while the physical presence is gone, the connections forged in life endure.

It's important to acknowledge challenges and skepticism regarding the belief in consciousness after death. The lack of empirical evidence and the subjective nature of personal experiences make it difficult to establish definitive conclusions. Alternative explanations rooted in psychology or neuroscience may account for phenomena interpreted as evidence of continuation. Engaging with these challenges fosters a balanced perspective, encouraging critical thinking and openness to multiple viewpoints.

Integrating beliefs about death and consciousness into daily life involves balancing conviction with humility. Respecting diverse views promotes empathy and constructive dialogue. Remaining curious and open to new information allows for growth and refinement of understanding. Ultimately, embracing life fully, regardless of what lies beyond, enriches the human experience and fosters a sense of connection and purpose.

Practical steps to engage with death and consciousness include reflective practices such as meditation on mortality, which can cultivate appreciation for the present moment and clarify priorities. Journaling about thoughts and feelings regarding death provides a space to explore personal beliefs and fears. Spiritual exploration through studying sacred texts or participating in rituals offers insights into various traditions and philosophies. Engaging in conversations with others and seeking support through groups or counseling can alleviate isolation and deepen understanding.

Ethical living, aligned with one's values and beliefs about the soul's journey, emphasizes kindness, integrity, and contribution to the greater good. Acts of service and compassion create a positive legacy that endures beyond physical existence. By focusing on personal growth and the impact of our actions, we honor the potential continuation of consciousness and the interconnectedness of all beings.

In conclusion, contemplating death, dying, and consciousness is a profound journey that touches the core of human existence. I believe that consciousness transcends the physical realm, continuing or transitioning to somewhere or someplace after death. This perspective shapes how I understand life, purpose, and the connections I share with others. Death, from this viewpoint, is not an absolute end but a passage to another state of being. It invites us to consider the possibilities that lie beyond and to live with intention and compassion.

Whether consciousness continues in a recognizable form, merges with a universal essence, or embarks on a new journey, the mystery of what lies beyond remains a source of wonder and reflection. By embracing the uncertainty and exploring diverse perspectives, we can find meaning and comfort in the face of mortality. The contemplation of death encourages us to value each moment, nurture our relationships, and contribute to the world in meaningful ways.

Ultimately, death is a universal experience that unites all living beings. Recognizing the potential continuation of consciousness offers hope and a sense of connection that transcends the boundaries of life and death. It reminds us that we are part of a greater tapestry of existence, woven together by the threads of experience, growth, and the eternal journey of the soul. Embracing this perspective enriches our lives, fosters empathy, and deepens our understanding of the profound mystery that is consciousness.

Conclusion: Consciousness as an Endless Journey

The exploration of consciousness is akin to embarking on an infinite voyage—a journey that transcends the boundaries of the known and ventures into the realms of the mysterious and the profound. Throughout this book, we have delved into the multifaceted nature of consciousness, examining its intricate relationship with the universe, the mind, the body, and the soul. As we arrive at the culmination of this exploration, it is both an opportunity and a necessity to synthesize the insights gained, reflect deeply on the themes discussed, and contemplate the future directions of our understanding of consciousness.

The Multifaceted Nature of Consciousness

Consciousness is not a monolithic entity but a complex tapestry woven from countless threads of experience, perception, thought, and emotion. It is the lens through which we perceive reality and the mirror that reflects our innermost selves. Throughout the chapters, we have seen that consciousness manifests in various dimensions—ranging from the individual subjective experiences to the collective consciousness that binds societies and cultures.

At the individual level, consciousness encompasses our thoughts, feelings, sensations, and awareness of self. It is the intimate experience of being alive, the stream of subjective experiences that defines our existence. This personal consciousness is dynamic and ever-changing, influenced by our interactions with the environment, our relationships, and our inner reflections.

On a broader scale, collective consciousness emerges from the shared beliefs, values, and norms of a group or society. It influences cultural evolution, social dynamics, and the progression of human civilization. This collective aspect of consciousness highlights the interconnectedness of individuals and underscores the impact of shared experiences and collective memory on the development of societies.

Consciousness and the Universe

One of the central themes we have explored is the profound relationship between consciousness and the universe. The notion that consciousness might be a fundamental aspect of reality, woven into the very fabric of the cosmos, challenges conventional scientific paradigms and opens new avenues for understanding existence.

The concept of panpsychism suggests that consciousness is not exclusive to humans or even living beings but is a fundamental feature of all matter. This perspective posits that every particle in the universe possesses some form of consciousness, however rudimentary. Such a view bridges the gap between the physical and the mental, offering a holistic understanding of reality where mind and matter are not separate but intertwined.

Quantum theories of consciousness further delve into the mysterious interplay between the observer and the observed. The role of the observer in quantum mechanics, where the act of measurement influences the state of a system, raises intriguing questions about the nature of reality and the influence of consciousness on the physical world. These theories suggest that consciousness may not merely be a passive witness to the unfolding of the universe but an active participant in shaping it.

The Anthropic Principle adds another layer to this discussion by proposing that the universe's fundamental constants are finely tuned to allow for the emergence of conscious observers. This idea invites contemplation on whether consciousness is an accidental byproduct of cosmic evolution or a fundamental component that the universe is structured to produce.

The Interconnectedness of All Things

A recurring motif throughout our exploration is the interconnectedness of all things. Consciousness serves as a bridge linking the self to the other, the individual to the collective, and humanity to the cosmos. This interconnectedness is not merely a philosophical abstraction but has practical implications for how we perceive ourselves and interact with the world.

In Eastern philosophies, such as Buddhism and Hinduism, the concept of interconnectedness is central. The idea of non-duality, where the distinction between self and other dissolves, emphasizes that all beings are part of a unified whole. Practices like meditation and mindfulness cultivate awareness of this interconnectedness, fostering compassion, empathy, and a sense of unity with all existence.

From an ecological perspective, recognizing the interconnectedness of all life forms encourages stewardship of the environment and sustainable living. Understanding that our actions impact not only ourselves but the entire web of life motivates ethical considerations and responsible behavior toward the planet.

Consciousness and Healing

The relationship between consciousness and healing underscores the power of the mind in influencing physical health and well-being. Throughout the chapters, we have examined how heightened levels of consciousness can enhance healing capacities, both perceived and actual.

Mind-body practices such as mindfulness meditation, yoga, and visualization techniques demonstrate that the mind can influence physiological processes. These practices reduce stress, improve immune function, and promote overall well-being. The placebo effect, where belief in a treatment's efficacy leads to real physiological improvements, further exemplifies the mind's influence on the body.

Embracing consciousness as a tool for healing extends beyond individual health. It fosters a holistic approach that considers emotional, mental, and spiritual dimensions. Healing becomes not just the alleviation of symptoms but a journey toward wholeness and integration of all aspects of the self.

The Philosophy of Mind

Delving into the philosophy of mind, we have grappled with questions about the nature of consciousness and its relationship to the physical brain. The debate between dualism and physicalism highlights the complexities of understanding consciousness.

Dualism posits that mind and body are distinct substances, with consciousness existing independently of physical processes. This perspective resonates with intuitive experiences of subjective awareness that seem irreducible to neural activity. It aligns with beliefs in the soul or spirit and supports concepts of life after death.

Physicalism, on the other hand, asserts that consciousness arises solely from physical processes in the brain. Advances in neuroscience have illuminated correlations between brain activity and mental states, suggesting that consciousness is an emergent property of complex neural networks.

While both perspectives offer valuable insights, the true nature of consciousness may lie beyond the dichotomy of dualism and physicalism. Integrative approaches consider consciousness as a fundamental aspect of reality, neither purely physical nor entirely separate from matter.

Consciousness in Eastern Philosophies

Eastern philosophies provide rich frameworks for understanding consciousness. Practices rooted in Buddhism and Hinduism emphasize direct experiential knowledge over conceptual understanding. Meditation, mindfulness, and self-inquiry are tools for transcending ordinary consciousness and realizing the true nature of the self.

In Buddhism, the concept of emptiness (Shunyata) teaches that all phenomena are interdependent and lack inherent existence. Recognizing this leads to the dissolution of the ego and liberation from suffering. The cultivation of compassion (Karuna) and loving-kindness (Metta) arises naturally from this understanding.

Hinduism introduces the idea of Atman (the inner self) and Brahman (the ultimate reality). The realization that Atman and Brahman are one leads to self-realization and enlightenment. Practices such as yoga, chanting, and rituals facilitate this realization by purifying the mind and aligning the individual with the divine.

These philosophies highlight that consciousness is not confined to the mind but permeates all existence. They offer pathways for expanding consciousness and experiencing unity with the cosmos.

Creativity and Consciousness

Creativity is a profound expression of consciousness. It is the act of bringing into existence something new and valuable, a manifestation of the mind's boundless potential. Higher levels of consciousness enhance creativity by opening channels to deeper insights, intuitive knowledge, and universal truths.

The creative process often involves entering a state of flow, where self-consciousness fades, and one becomes fully immersed in the activity. This state is marked by heightened awareness, clarity, and joy. Practices that elevate consciousness, such as meditation and mindfulness, facilitate access to flow states.

Understanding creativity as a co-creative process with the divine or the universal mind adds a spiritual dimension. It positions the individual not merely as an originator but as a conduit for creative energy that transcends personal limitations. This perspective imbues creative endeavors with purpose and aligns them with the greater good.

Death, Dying, and Consciousness

Contemplating death and what lies beyond is an intrinsic part of exploring consciousness. Beliefs about death influence how we live, perceive the self, and understand the journey of consciousness.

The idea that consciousness transcends physical death offers solace and a sense of continuity. It frames death as a transition or continuation rather than an absolute end. Concepts like reincarnation, the afterlife, or merging with a universal consciousness provide narratives that give meaning to the cycle of life and death.

Near-death experiences and accounts of past-life memories challenge materialistic views that consciousness ceases with brain activity. While empirical evidence is elusive, these phenomena invite open-minded inquiry into the nature of consciousness and its potential to exist beyond physical form.

Embracing the mystery of death encourages us to live authentically, value relationships, and pursue personal growth. It fosters acceptance of life's impermanence and inspires actions that reflect our deepest values.

Ethical and Existential Implications

Understanding consciousness has profound ethical and existential implications. Recognizing the interconnectedness of all beings promotes compassion, empathy, and ethical responsibility. It challenges us to consider the impact of our actions on others and the environment.

Conscious living involves aligning actions with values that honor the sanctity of life and the well-being of all. It encourages mindful consumption, sustainable practices, and social justice. By elevating consciousness, we become agents of positive change, contributing to a more harmonious and equitable world.

The Role of Science and Spirituality

Integrating scientific inquiry with spiritual wisdom enriches our understanding of consciousness. Science offers methodologies for exploring the physical correlates of consciousness, while spirituality provides insights into subjective experiences and the transcendent aspects of existence.

Interdisciplinary approaches bridge the gap between objective and subjective realms. Fields like neurotheology study the neural basis of spiritual experiences, while contemplative neuroscience examines the effects of meditation on the brain. These collaborations expand the scope of research and open new possibilities for understanding consciousness.

Acknowledging the limitations of both science and spirituality fosters humility and openness. It invites a collaborative exploration that respects empirical evidence and honors personal experiences.

Embracing Uncertainty and the Mystery

Consciousness remains one of the greatest mysteries. Despite advancements in various fields, definitive answers elude us. Embracing uncertainty is not a resignation but an invitation to continuous exploration.

The mystery of consciousness encourages curiosity, wonder, and a sense of adventure. It reminds us that the journey is as important as the destination. By accepting that some aspects may remain unknowable, we cultivate patience and appreciation for the unfolding of understanding over time.

The Endless Journey

Consciousness is an endless journey—dynamic, evolving, and boundless. Each individual's exploration is unique, shaped by personal experiences, cultural influences, and innate curiosity. Collectively, our journeys contribute to the expanding tapestry of human understanding.

As we navigate this journey, several guiding principles emerge:

- **Openness to Experience:** Embrace new ideas, perspectives, and experiences. Remain receptive to learning from others and from the world around us.
- **Reflective Practice:** Engage in self-inquiry, meditation, and mindfulness to deepen self-awareness and connect with the inner self.
- **Compassion and Empathy:** Cultivate kindness toward oneself and others. Recognize the shared humanity and interconnectedness of all beings.
- **Ethical Action:** Align actions with values that promote well-being, justice, and harmony. Act with integrity and responsibility.
- **Creative Expression:** Utilize creativity as a means of exploration and communication. Allow it to be a vehicle for personal growth and societal contribution.
- **Acceptance of Mystery:** Acknowledge the unknown and the unknowable. Let it inspire awe and humility.

Looking Forward

The future of consciousness exploration holds immense potential. Advancements in technology, neuroscience, psychology, and philosophy will continue to shed light on the workings of the mind. Interdisciplinary collaborations will foster innovative approaches and discoveries.

At the same time, the integration of ancient wisdom and contemporary science offers a holistic framework. Practices that have stood the test of time, such as meditation and mindfulness, will remain valuable tools for personal and collective growth.

Emerging fields like artificial intelligence and virtual reality raise new questions about consciousness. Can machines possess consciousness? How will technology influence human consciousness? These inquiries will shape ethical considerations and societal developments.

Global challenges, such as environmental crises, social inequality, and cultural conflicts, call for elevated consciousness. Addressing these issues requires empathy, collaboration, and a recognition of our shared destiny. Consciousness exploration becomes not just an individual pursuit but a collective imperative.

Final Reflections

As we conclude this journey through the landscapes of consciousness, it is evident that the quest to understand the mind, the self, and the universe is as infinite as consciousness itself. The insights gained are stepping stones, guiding us toward deeper understanding and more meaningful existence.

Consciousness is the essence of who we are—the core of our being that perceives, feels, thinks, and knows. It is the thread that connects us to each other and to the cosmos. Exploring consciousness enriches our lives, expands our horizons, and empowers us to live authentically.

I invite you to continue this exploration with curiosity and openness. Embrace the practices that resonate with you, engage with ideas that challenge you, and connect with others on this shared journey. Remember that every moment is an opportunity to awaken to deeper levels of consciousness.

May this journey inspire you to live with purpose, compassion, and joy. May it lead you to discover the boundless potential within and the profound connections that unite us all.

Milton Keynes UK
Ingram Content Group UK Ltd.
UKHW021920151124
451262UK00014B/1521